Reinventing and Reinvesting
in the Local
for Our Common Good

Reinventing and Reinvesting in the Local for Our Common Good

Edited by

Brian A. Hoey

Selected Papers from the Annual Meeting of the
Southern Anthropological Society,
Huntington, West Virginia
April, 2016

Betty J. Duggan
SAS Proceedings Interim Series Editor

Newfound Press
THE UNIVERSITY OF TENNESSEE LIBRARIES, KNOXVILLE

Southern Anthropological Society
Founded 1966

Reinventing and Reinvesting in the Local for Our Common Good
© 2020 by Southern Anthropological Society: *southernanthro.org*

Print on demand available through University of Tennessee Press.
DOI: https://doi.org/10.7290/vx8shbx

For all other uses, contact:
Newfound Press
University of Tennessee Libraries
1015 Volunteer Boulevard
Knoxville, TN 37996-1000
newfoundpress.utk.edu

ISBN-13: 978-0-9860803-6-4 (paperback)
ISBN-13: 978-0-9860803-7-1 (PDF)

Names: Hoey, Brian A., 1968- author, editor. | Southern Anthropological Society.
    Meeting (2016 : Huntington, West Virginia) | Marshall University, host institution.
Title: Reinventing and reinvesting in the local for our common good / edited by Brian
    A. Hoey.
Description: Knoxville, Tennessee : Newfound Press, University of Tennessee
    Libraries, [2020] | 1 online resource (192 pages) : color illustrations | Series:
    Southern Anthropological Society proceedings ; no. 44 | Includes bibliographical
    references. | Summary: "Selected Papers from the Annual Meeting of the Southern
    Anthropological Society, Huntington, West Virginia, April, 2016"—Title page.
Identifiers: ISBN-13: 978-0-9860803-7-1 (PDF) | ISBN-13: 978-0-9860803-6-4
    (paperback)
Subjects: LCSH: Applied anthropology—Congresses. | Community organization—
    Southern States—Case studies—Congresses. | Common good—Case studies—
    Congresses. | Social change—Southern States—Case studies—Congresses. |
    Mass media in health education—Botswana—Case studies—Congresses. | HIV
    (Viruses)—Botswana—Prevention—Congresses. | AIDS (Disease)—Botswana—
    Prevention—Congresses. | Teenage girls—Health and hygiene—Botswana—
    Congresses. | American students—South Africa—Cross-cultural studies—
    Congresses. | Autistic people—Services for—Congresses.
Classification: LCC GN560.U6 (PDF) | LCC GN560.U6 R45 2020 (print)

Book design by Martha Rudolph
Cover design and photograph by C. S. Jenkins

Contents

Connecting, Exchanging, and Having Impact

Brian A. Hoey and Hannah G. Smith

Engaged Anthropology

Anthropologists have long been committed to social science done in public and in the public interest. This commitment has been demonstrated by, among other things, support for a globally contextualized understanding of local-level processes of change—a history considered in this volume in the chapter by Melinda Wagner and in Brian Hoey's personal reflection on the ethnographic method. Despite this long-standing commitment, anthropology has only infrequently reached public consciousness and discussion, even while ideas and practices native to the discipline have been put to use fruitfully by other scholars as well as various practitioners working in the public domain. These non-anthropologists have, at times, been more willing and able to expand the impact of core concepts and methods native to anthropology than have anthropologists themselves. Speaking to fellow anthropologists as the field emerged from at least twenty years of roiling (and often divisive) introspection that seemed to leave many within the discipline averse to practical engagement, James Peacock noted that "If the discipline is to gain recognition and a valuable identity, it must accomplish things; it must be active beyond its analytical strategy. Pragmatism and searching critique need not be mutually exclusive" (Peacock 1997, 12).

In order to be relevant, anthropology needs to be seen—perhaps as it once was in the mid-twentieth century—as a publicly-involved field offering valuable methodological, conceptual, and analytical resources to those who develop and assess policies that affect every-day lives. We see an illustration of such valuation in the chapter by Adams and Damron in this volume in which they address developing an appreciation of neurodiversity through deliberate change in prevailing cultural values. At the same time, the field should be accessible to those who might put these valuable resources—freely available from within the methodological and conceptual "toolkits" of the anthropologist—to work in offering locally-grounded and effective alternatives to mainstream programs, to fill consequential gaps in knowledge and/or service, and to otherwise seek to improve their own circumstances through thoughtful, grassroots action. Anthropology and anthropologists, together with their ideas and approaches, have much to offer people who work for various forms of cultural and social change. Our offerings include an ability to document and describe how broad, macro-level policy may impact local-level conditions as well as how, potentially, the reverse may take place. Some of this work will have an academic audience, of course, but we must also recognize how we may be called to help describe and explain what are often complex, multifaceted, and extra-local factors that affect local communities to residents of these places who genuinely want and need our help. Our role must go beyond providing indirect support by virtue of the value of our theory and methods as supplies to be virtually "handed out." Anthropologists must also be seen as enthusiastic and humble allies who are directly engaged in collaborative actions such as suggested in the chapter by Hoey in this volume. These collaborations may be multi-disciplinary partnerships born of the academy or emergent within community-based alliances created out of the immediate needs of persons for whom the output of academics may appear largely, if not completely, irrelevant to popular efforts to solve local problems.

Perhaps the most publicly recognized anthropologist of all time, a woman who worked in many cultural contexts around the world during the mid-twentieth century, Margaret Mead lends a succinct statement to capture the discipline's ongoing sense of the possibility of meaningful change through committed, practical engagement by saying, simply, that we should "Never doubt that a small group of thoughtful, committed citizens can change the world; indeed, it is the only thing that ever has."[1] In many ways, the essence of this assertion was the point of departure for our efforts to come together first at the 51st Annual Meetings of the Southern Anthropological Society (SAS) and now in these Proceedings.

Our Theme and Process

The state of West Virginia faces many challenges. These are born of continuing factors such as economic restructuring as well as acute crises that include, for example, a chemical spill into the drinking water of over three hundred thousand residents in 2014 and devastating floods that struck just months before our April 2016 SAS conference in Huntington, West Virginia. In the past several years, public health crises such as substance abuse (particularly opioid addiction) have ravaged communities in West Virginia as they have throughout Appalachia and beyond.

In planning for the conference and in our effort to pull together this volume of work, we chose to face such challenges by engaging with each other to "reinvent our local." This engagement involved recognizing the enduring value of collective heritage together with an eye toward purposefully creating a promising future through reinvestment in shared quality of life. Our commitment to "the local" as manifest in the discrete communities that serve as the consequential places for our working and personal lives is in no way a turning away from recognition of the multitude of ways in which any such place is embedded within a web of networks that must respond to tensions created by extra-local forces. Indeed, these forces, including far-reaching economic and environmental policies and phenomena, test taken-for-granted ways of doing things in any given corner of the world. Rather, the organizing principle at work behind the conference and Proceedings recognizes that we are each situated as persons and practitioners—whether more or less academic or applied in our professional positions—within distinct places that face their own set of challenges and opportunities. This is to say, the anthropologically-minded research presented at the Southern Anthropological Society conference in 2016 and within this volume is done in the interests of both a personal and public good. We recognize that each of us is part of a common good which we are collectively responsible for creating and maintaining. Thus, our focus on locally-engaged work is much more than simply a means of molding or modifying a research agenda. Rather it becomes a model for informing our own life-long learning, our mentoring within multiple contexts (not simply the classroom), and, of course, the actions we take as citizens.

A cultural anthropologist at Marshall University, Hoey's most recent research has built on earlier work examining acts of everyday place-making as well as deliberate place-marketing as he explores the cultural construction of Appalachia as a distinct region. This research considers how the literature of Appalachian studies intersects the work of scholars interested in postindustrial economic restructuring and its consequences for economic growth and community development by documenting the efforts of activists and others who attempt to redefine the sources and meaning of economic growth in West Virginia. Based in Huntington, home to Marshall University, Hoey has observed and participated in local efforts to establish a purposeful narrative of place with which to animate efforts to reinvent and reinvest in his own local through such groups as Create Huntington on whose board he served. Create Huntington is an instrumental, home-grown actor that grew out of coordinated efforts of motivated residents, Marshall University, and the City mayor's office. Beginning in 2006, this forward-looking citizen-based organization, which received charitable 501(c)(3) non-profit status in early 2010, has worked to facilitate development of a what is termed a "vision for progress" among community members and to apply these ideas in Huntington and the surrounding area. As stated in a 2009 interview with Hoey, Thomas McChesney, founding organization board member and native to the area, Create Huntington exists "to provide the structure to enable creatives to do what they think is important, not to tell them what is important. That is something that has become a competitive disadvantage for the area because for too long people here have been told what they should think and what is important" (personal communication, June 2009).

The conference provided numerous examples of how Huntington is committed as a community to progressively reinventing and re-investing in the local after years of decline in the coal-sector and old manufacturing economies. Work by the City of Huntington, as presented by city planner Breanna Shell, outlined core initiatives documented in a comprehensive revitalization plan known as the Huntington Innovation Project (HIP), which depended on the extensive collaboration of multiple stakeholders. The HIP plan was submitted to the America's Best Communities competition, and Huntington won the competition in 2017. The plan includes strategies to redevelop vacant industrial properties along the Ohio River near the Marshall University campus—once the manufacturing center of the town's railroad roots—into new recreational and riverfront amenities; retail and hotel development; green infrastructure for storm water management; and a world-class technology commercialization and advanced manufacturing center. Also included in the plan is an extension of work begun in the West End of Huntington where the City is assisting the non-profit Coalfield Development Corporation in redeveloping a 96,000-square-foot former garment factory into a social enterprise center known as WestEdge. When complete, the facility will have the largest solar roof in West Virginia, a solar training institute, a woodshop that up-cycles reclaimed materials into furniture, an indoor mushroom and microgreen growing operation, and other facilities and programs that will retrain workers displaced by economic restructuring in the Appalachian region through ReWire Appalachia. Initiatives such as these require strong partnerships such as those realized in successful efforts of Marshall University and the City to transform the 114-year-old

Anderson-Newcomb Building into the School of Art and Design's Visual Arts Center.

Through a 13.4-million-dollar renovation project, this six-story former department store, located squarely downtown and steps from the conference venue, was transformed into the state-of-the-art Marshall University Visual Arts Center where the School of Art and Design relocated from cramped and out-of-date facilities on campus in 2014. In 1902, the Visual Arts program started at Marshall. That same year, the historic Anderson-Newcomb Building was built on Third Avenue. For years, as a well-stocked department store, Anderson-Newcomb was central to the hustle and bustle of mid-twentieth century Huntington until completion of a shopping mall in 1981 just outside of the city shifted much economic and social activity away from downtown. Today, after extensive renovation, this building brings people to downtown Huntington by offering a unique arts experience to both students and citizens.

This historical landmark has become a showcase for how collaborative efforts to connect people to creatively exchange ideas can have lasting impact on the life of a community. The building design and its urban context stimulate synergy through a vibrant bridging between the University and various partners that results in course projects, program initiatives, and transformative student experiences that contribute to the quality of both individual and collective lives. When students leave the Visual Arts Center, they step immediately into an urban environment in which they are participating actively and contributing as citizens. As members of both the University community and the community of Huntington, students contribute to the reinvention of the city as a creative laboratory. Further, students develop skills that will last a lifetime as they complete internships with non-profit organizations and private businesses and participate in creative initiatives throughout the city.

The conference from which contributions to this volume were drawn was conceived as a direct and deliberate expression of Hoey's observation through experiences in Huntington and other field-work sites (ranging from the near Midwestern United States to far Southeast Asia) that people from all walks of life can achieve great things when they choose to come together to share their hopes and dreams, exchange ideas, build on the skills that each brings, and take supported action designed to have real impact for a common good. Connect. Exchange. Impact. The conference—just as this volume—was titled "Reinventing and Reinvesting in the Local for Our Common Good" and entailed numerous efforts to brand and reflect this theme through organized sessions, workshops, and field-trips, as well as in such details as signage and social media outreach.

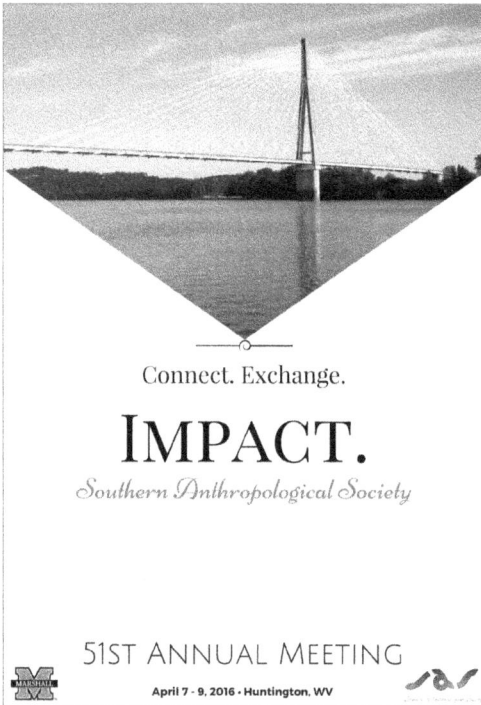

Connect. Exchange.

IMPACT.

Southern Anthropological Society

51ST ANNUAL MEETING

April 7 - 9, 2016 · Huntington, WV

This vision was invoked in our choice of a landmark, a prominent local bridge for our conference posters, a detail you will see reflected in the Wagner chapter where it serves as a kind of trope. We saw our coming together for the two days of this conference, and beyond, as a bridging between what are too often practically separated domains—institutions of higher learning and their larger communities.

As a professional academic, Hoey has endeavored to challenge colleagues within and outside his disciplinary home of anthropology to envision ways that an engaged, public scholarship can contribute directly and significantly to improving the common good within the communities where we live and work.

Among the conference program highlights, attendees had the opportunity to enjoy and engage in research presented on an array of diverse topics such as those presented in this volume. There were also workshops and panels on topics including service learning and other pedagogical subjects that aimed to reinvigorate the work of attendees in and out of the classroom; historical preservation in a local, state, and federal regulatory environment; "smart growth" through application of social science-based evidence; and emerging water crises. Through collaboration with the Marshall University College of Arts and Media, we also benefitted from lively discussion surrounding an art installation prepared by graduating "capstone" students within the fine arts that spoke in a variety of compelling ways to the conference theme.

(Photo courtesy of Lori Wolfe, *The Herald-Dispatch*, Huntington, West Virginia)

Live music and creative performances over three days expressed our conference theme in different ways, including a Welcome "After Party" on Thursday night that featured the local American roots music band Big Rock and the Candy Ass Mountain Boys. Tours and fieldtrips highlighted local examples of reinvention and reinvestment such as the Visual Arts Center for a glimpse of how "town and gown" were united in the renovation of a dilapidated but once glorious downtown building. Conference goers also had the chance to tour the Keith Albee Theatre, a 1928 Thomas Lamb masterpiece of the vaudeville era and one of the few remaining examples of this extraordinary architectural work nationwide. Located at the edge of the city, the Heritage Farm Museum and Village (HFMV), recently named one of very few Affiliate sites of the Smithsonian Institute, allowed visitors to experience a wide array of collections as well as a living history feature that highlights long-standing achievements of Appalachians who have faced myriad challenges living through hard times. Principle among the lessons offered at HFMV—and one that frankly counters prevailing stereotypes of Appalachia—is that not only are the people of the region distinctive for their strong-willed dedication to tradition but also for their extraordinary degree of ingenuity and innovation. Fortunately for all, this latter trait has kept many residents resiliently open to the kinds of broadminded ideas highlighted in this volume. We can turn to the internationally recognized work of the West Virginia Autism Training Center, located in Huntington, which provides services to persons on the autism spectrum (as described in the Adams and Damron chapter), as an apt illustration of such local innovation and open-mindedness.

In order to bring the conference to fruition and thus lay the foundations for this volume, Hoey worked with six extraordinary student-interns under the auspices of the SAS who envisioned it not as a cloistered gathering of academics—as is so often the case for such events—but rather as a dynamic, open meeting space intended to purposefully connect academics and non-academics in an exchange of experiences, ideas, and plans that could lead us to have positive impact in our communities. Throughout the semester, students Heidi Dennison, Jake Farley, Samantha Harvey, Alexis Kastigar, Hannah Smith, and Jocelyn Taylor had a behind-the-scenes experience learning how to host an academic conference. From field trips and activities to advertising, these students were actively involved in all aspects of conference planning. This experience was envisioned by Hoey as a chance for participation in publicly-engaged scholarship in a way not possible in a traditional classroom setting. They gained knowledge and experience beneficial in future endeavors that require an active, collaborative engagement through planning and execution of a multifaceted event. In addition to their involvement in planning the conference, they presented individual work in a group-organized session. They were, in fact, fully involved in the conference—both behind and on the stage.

In the fall semester of 2015, Hoey approached his co-author on this chapter, Hannah Smith (who was then pursuing her undergraduate degrees as an anthropology and biochemistry double-major) with the opportunity to help plan while receiving class credit. As might be expected of a sophomore in college, she knew little about planning an academic conference. Nevertheless, she jumped at the opportunity. As a result, Smith—and ultimately five other students who would join her—learned more about anthropology as a discipline as well as community engagement as an investment in the future and a common good. As participants in this internship course, students were simultaneously learning from their professor while collaborating with student peers as co-workers to develop a successful conference. Engaging in robust conversations and contributing individual ideas to a collective project challenged them to bring distinct viewpoints for considering, among other things, how to define "the local" of Huntington. Huntington served as our starting point and the common ground on which to share ideas based on our varied as well as shared experiences. Much as in the conference, Huntington as both place and subject became the site where our viewpoints came together.

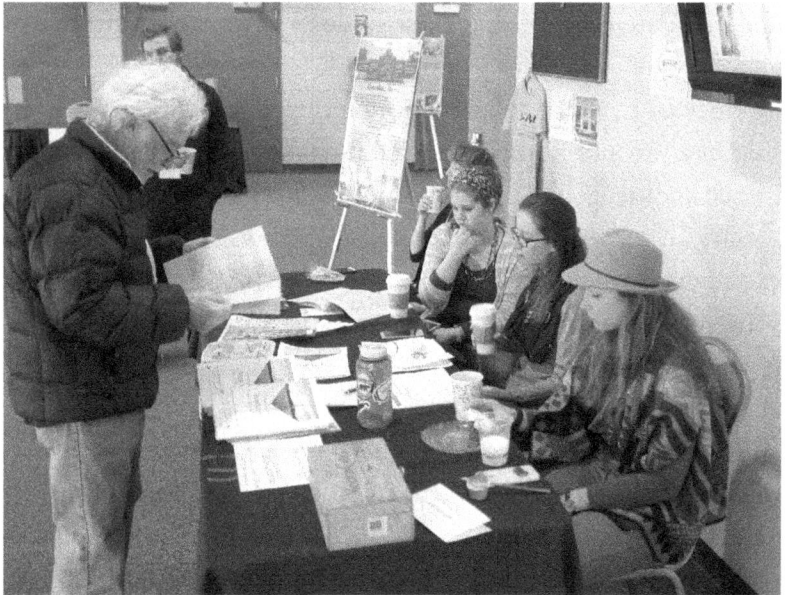

The dual perspective of this internship course created an interesting dynamic. Because Smith was experiencing analytical and methodological approaches basic to anthropology firsthand, she actively learned the discipline while simultaneously engaging in her local community. Never had she seen "a small group of thoughtful, committed citizens" more driven than the activists she encountered in Huntington while preparing for the conference as well as in her historical research into the economic and cultural history of the city for a paper Smith presented at the SAS conference titled "From Industrialism to Tourism: A Look at Cultural and Economic Changes in Huntington, West Virginia." Huntington's economy boomed with industrialization in the early twentieth century. As factories shuttered, thousands of jobs for blue-collar workers came to an abrupt end, generally without immediate alternatives. Huntington's community leaders and its citizens have had to adapt to an economic reality shaped by global forces manifesting at the local level. Becoming involved in her local through the eyes of an anthropologist reignited Smith's passion for this place and its people. And this was the goal of the conference as a whole: for attendees to come away with visions of what they might do at home, in their own local, that would contribute to a common good.

Engaging with her community as an anthropologist also allowed Smith to become deeply mindful of the changes that it was experiencing. Growing up just outside of Huntington, she was imprecisely aware of the extent of problems facing the community. Beyond research for her paper, simply making phone calls to schedule conference field trips made her more aware of the social, cultural, and economic particulars of the community. In her active participation in varied sectors of life in Huntington, Smith was not simply a social scientist searching for answers (and donations to help fund the conference), but a resident hoping for a better future. Once the conference commenced, Smith and her fellow students interacted with people from a variety of backgrounds from several states. As attendees shared their work and spoke passionately of its impact in their own local, the students learned how both old and new ideas can be incorporated into community planning so as to reinvent and reinvest in the local for the welfare of all.

Now studying to receive her Masters of Environmental Management at Duke University, Smith attributes her ability to communicate effectively across disciplines and between community members— which is the crux of environmental management—to her undergraduate experience in anthropology. Through this experience, she learned firsthand that she is at once a citizen and an academic with responsibility to foster sustainable solutions for problems that affect the environment. Change occurs when individuals with unique backgrounds share a passion for a common local.

Discussion of Themes as Manifest in the Chapters

Though a small volume, the reader will encounter a rich diversity of material compellingly presented across chapters that each contribute in their own distinct way to the collection by illustrating, through their differences, a series of shared themes. At some points, these themes are purposefully referenced as linkages to those explicitly stated as foundational to the conference and volume. At other times, readers will be able to make their own meaningful connections by applying an understanding of the ideas already discussed that motivated organizers of the conference.

Among these chapters, the reader will discover many instances of how our authors seek their own research and experientially-driven ways of contributing to public policy. We see how each is interested in how policies and practices affecting the public, often at the national or even global level, may or may not work within local circumstances. Local conditions may constitute what are described by anthropologists as culturally-particular contexts. "Top-down" policy is characteristically insensitive to viable, though what might be described as "unconventional," approaches. For instance, Upton speaks of messages from media with global origins that may encourage cross-generational sex to young girls in Botswana. She argues that an effective means to combat the effects of such negative influence is to address the problem with locally-informed initiatives and conversations. Wagner echoes this sentiment. When a community is empowered to communicate amongst itself in a search for answers, emergent solutions are locally relevant where a would-be solution imposed—good intentions and all—from outside may fail for the lack of relevance and what many community activists would describe as "buy in" or, simply, a sense of ownership by local people.

We see our authors each striving to establish the need for what might be deemed "alternatives" to status quo ways of doing things at multiple levels and domains ranging from a variety of extant public policies to common practices among those who have significant influence on the everyday lives of others, including educators such as those that have contributed to this volume. Part and parcel of this effort is establishing how the efficacy of a particular policy may depend to a great extent on making that policy or education locally pertinent, compelling, meaningful or, perhaps, itself driven by both people and ideas at the local level. Thus, we might make connections here to principles of "cultural competence" when it comes to what some characterize as "intervention," at a minimum, or more extensively as "grassroots" forms of development that shape quality of life for local people in ways that they can and should determine more fully for themselves. We also find reference among the chapters to local cultural reinterpretations of extra-local messages and practices. In all, we are ever reminded of the essential fact that the local, or what might be referred to as "community," serves as the site for meaningful, substantive change in people's lives. It is where lives are, in fact, lived.

Not surprisingly, here we are given entrée to a variety of illustrations for how *ethnography* serves as an essential methodology for allowing social scientists to more completely understand issues that motivate people by giving shape and meaning to their experience. Chapters from Wagner and Hoey, in particular, speak to this point. Importantly, in ways that we see discussed within this volume, ethnographically-informed social science and the public policy that may emerge from it are only part of our concern. Ethnographic engagement constitutes a means of relationship and community-building.

Here we may point to a commitment to mutual understanding born of this methodology that helps create a kind of "shared" or even what some have characterized as a "safe" space out of a co-organized melding of individual experiences and distinct understandings of the world. Shaped by the background of different developmental environments, each person carries his or her own local. By engaging people of different circumstances and creating spaces that foster relationships, distinct communities of experience may merge to form an entirely new shared "local" where unique perspectives combine with the potential to solve problems through helping to visualize and, perhaps then realize, a common good.

Simply stated, communication—beginning with the desire to know a person from whom we might, without that determination for insight, set ourselves apart—becomes the bridge by which we access the ideas and feelings of others in order to reach this shared good. As examined in detail in the chapter by Hoey, ethnographic approaches provide people with the exceptional opportunity to wear hats of both participant and observer, as the role is commonly understood. As practiced by anthropologists, in particular, ethnography allows everyone the potential to be like a student, open to learning. The chapters in this volume exemplify how each member of a relationship becomes a student of others. For example, London and Klaaren's South African peer-educators learned as much from American students visiting the country during a study-aboard experience as the Americans did from their peer-educators. The core reason for the mutual learning experience described by London and Klaaren was the dynamic space for dialogue the course provided, even though this space emerged as an unintended outcome of the encounter between distinct groups of students. In their chapter, Adams and Damron speak to the varied ways of knowing that are realized in the fundamental fact of human neurodiversity and how, specifically, those on the autism spectrum may be empowered to share valuable insight and experience with the communities where they live and beyond. As long as individuals work to understand unique forms of communication enacted by neurodiverse individuals, the collective mindset of society can change in ways that open up rewarding possibilities for everyone.

London and Klaaren, together with Adams and Damron, provide compelling instances of "reciprocal learning" and its potential for positive outcomes for all involved. In the end, an engaged anthropological approach centers on relationships and, in particular, seeks to understand connections between individual persons, actors, and larger social collectives from the local to the global and to see how these connections shape meaning for people. What drives people's actions or motivates their desires? As stated in Upton, what are significant "cultural drivers" of different behaviors and in what precise ways would knowing these serve in making policy or programs intended to improve the lives of people in particular times and places?

Honest conversations bring to light both meaningful differences and shared experiences and desires. As Wagner suggests, relationship building in such conversations helps the world become at least a little bit safer for human difference. This transformation occurs by virtue of the effort to construct rapport and arrive at mutual trust in a manner fundamental to the ethnographic method and, in particular, collaborative approaches of a truly engaged anthropology. Adams and Damron speak to benefits conferred by such open conversations about diversity generally and, specifically, neurodiversity. London and Klaaren show how being open about diversity allows individuals to adjust beliefs and practices. As each individual perspective shifts, so might a collective mindset within a community. Upton speaks to the impact of global ideals on a community, both positive and negative. In much the same way as London and Klaaren,

Upton's research describes how open dialogue within a community can serve as a catalyst to spark change in the lives of individuals. Individuals may influence the community as much as the local influences each person. Therefore, an emerging theme in each chapter is the importance of communication and involvement between committed individuals to shape a common local.

NOTES

1. This statement is attributed to Margaret Mead. Though it is clearly consistent with her statements regarding activism, there is no written record of it. Hence, no citation to provide.

WORKS CITED

Peacock, James L. 1997. "The Future of Anthropology." *American Anthropologist* 99 (1): 9-17.

Celebrating the Local*

Melinda Bollar Wagner

This chapter is a cheerleading pep rally, a game plan, and the beginnings of a how-to-do-it instruction manual for "engaged" local anthropology. It assumes a beginner's knowledge, but the chapters in this volume demonstrate that scholars are bringing a wide variety of expertise and sophisticated activities into their local communities.

Engaged Anthropology in the Profession

On the one hand, historically anthropology could be said to have displayed some snobbery regarding local fieldwork, or even fieldwork within the USA. On the other hand, the work of distinguished forefathers and mothers includes numerous endorsements for the anthropology of the local. Margaret Mead's prolific writings included many in a popular genre, including articles for *Redbook* magazine (Gordan 1976). Margaret Mead's teacher Franz Boas, recognized as the founder of the discipline in the United States when he developed the doctoral program at Columbia University in the late 1890s, "wrote for, and spoke to, the public at large" (Blakey et al. 1994, 298). Margaret Mead's colleague Ruth Benedict, said, "The purpose of anthropology is to make the world safe for human differences."[1]

* Thank you to Mary LaLone for allowing me to use her work in this chapter and for many hours of conversation about how to make this work rigorous pedagogy that produces useful and sophisticated products.

Coming forward in time from Margaret Mead, we need look no further than some of the leading lights of anthropology for confirmation that we should be going local. Roy A. (Skip) Rappaport (1994, 245) advocated "engaged cultural anthropology" committed to "cultural pluralism and democratic participation." *Diagnosing America: Anthropology and Public Engagement*, edited by Shepard Forman (1994), includes chapters from nine anthropologists who formed the American Anthropological Association's Panel on Disorders of Industrial Societies, including two presidents of the American Anthropological Association, James Peacock and Roy Rappaport. The book ends with "A Statement to the Profession" by the panel that warns, "American anthropology stands at a crossroads. We have the opportunity to engage on the major social issues that are confronting our society, or we can remain peripheral to them . . . Anthropology grows narrower, more constricted in theme and purpose as we compete to serve our professional goals rather than direct the discipline toward the generation of knowledge that has some more useful purpose" (Blakey et al. 1994, 295, 297).

The American Anthropological Association encompasses forty sections and ten interest groups. Of those fifty, between fifteen to twenty percent are clearly applied. The Society for Applied Anthropology itself was founded in 1941. The National Association for the Practice of Anthropology began in 1983. In 2007, the American Anthropological Association added a standing Committee on Practicing, Applied and Public Interest Anthropology (CoPAPIA). The *American Anthropologist* added a section and editors for Practicing Anthropology in 2008 and Public Anthropology in 2010. The Public Anthropology section "charts the vast range of forms practicing anthropology is taking . . . Anthropologists are increasingly engaged in a vast range of communities and reaching numerous constituencies outside captive students and narrow academic scholarly circles"

(Wali, Checker, and Vine 2010, 638). The interest in "engaged anthropology" is substantiated by the explosion of articles in the last several years defining and analyzing it. *Collaborative Anthropologies* was launched in 2008. *Current Anthropology* devoted an issue to engaged anthropology in 2010 (Volume 51, Supplement 2, October 2010). Some authors are concerned about neoliberal universities co-opting engagement with communities (Checker 2014). Others describe ways they helped shaped their universities' centers and programs that promote university-community cooperation and engagement (Bennett and Whiteford 2013; Hyland and Bennett 2013; Hyland and Maurette 2010; Norris-Tirrell, Lambert-Pennington, and Hyland 2010; Whiteford and Strom 2013). Low and Merry (2010) developed a categorization of the various forms engaged anthropology can take. Granted, these writings are not all focused on engaging with LOCAL communities, which is the focus of this volume.

Engaged Anthropology in the Community

The hallmarks of the discipline of anthropology render anthropologists useful to local communities and organizations that need help with planning, data gathering, or communicating to power holders. We offer an internal/insiders' perspective; theories for what culture is and how it works; comparisons and alternatives; and systems analysis that views cultures as integrated parts, emphasizing that change in one part precipitates change in others. Our methods allow for learning about the cultural processes of various entities— schools, factories, organizations of all kinds. We need look no further than our own methods for how to proceed when working with local communities.

The theme of the Southern Anthropological Society's fifty-first annual meeting was "Reinventing and Reinvesting in the Local for Our Common Good," with the motto "Connect. Exchange. Impact."

The meeting's icon was the striking East Huntington Bridge, a 900-foot cable-stayed bridge over the Ohio River in Huntington, West Virginia. The bridge provides an acronym for the relationship between the academy and the community through local engagement.

Be a Bridge

B   Be willing to cross Boundaries

R   Reduce jargon; Relate; Communicate

I   Keep your Identity—pay attention to your community partners' Identity

D   Don't compromise your method or theory

G   Get Connected

E   Engage

Discussing these directives in a different order will allow us to successfully arrive at Getting Connected and Engaged.

D—Don't compromise your method or theory

A distinction is often drawn between basic research and applied research. However, when going local, there is no need to abandon our best ethnographic research methods. Researching an essay on methods, I queried anthropologists with wide-ranging field sites—in places far away, in dangerous places, in safe places, and in local places—about their fieldwork experiences. I heard very similar stories. It was not difficult to draw an overall picture of how fieldwork progresses, fieldwork's pitfalls, fieldwork's decisions and strategies. When going local, use anthropology's method and theory—but explain them to your constituents. Retain your research mode—but realize that your community partners might not share it.

A project undertaken with undergraduate anthropology students and residents of local counties in the New River Valley of Virginia provides an example of pedagogy, professionalism, pitfalls, and successes. The Power Line Project began in an Appalachian Studies Seminar with a class project focused on resistance in Appalachia. An example of ongoing resistance was occurring next door to the University—the controversy surrounding the proposal by Appalachian Power Company (ApCo, American Electric Power) to build a 765,000-volt power line from Oceana, West Virginia, to Cloverdale, Virginia. The 765s, as they are called, use power towers that are 8 stories high (132 feet) with 200-foot wide rights-of-way. This particular line would have 333 towers and stretch for 100 miles. The power line would "wheel" power generated in old coal-fired power plants (grandfathered by the Environmental Protection Agency) to the Atlantic coast, increasing power flow to eastern cities. It would cross rural mountainous counties of Appalachian Virginia and West Virginia. Some of the proposed routes would cross National Forest land.

Activists from this and earlier environmental controversies, power company executives, and academic experts on social movements and culture change visited the classroom. Then students met the protagonists on their home turf to interview them. The class created a twenty-five-page script for a simulated "town meeting," with students taking on the various roles in the debate. They impersonated local land-owning protesters, company personnel, and representatives from the National Forest and the Appalachian Trail, using their words, and feeling their emotions. A thirty-minute simultaneous video and slide show was developed from the scripted town meeting.

The sense of place versus the place of progress came head-to-head in residents' and power company's perspectives on the power line. Residents who came to the class said, "We are a thinly settled rural relatively poor area lying between surplus generation in the west and growth area in the east . . . They're making us a national sacrifice area . . . They're going to peddle power over us." The decisions regarding whether to build the power line, and if so, where, rested in the hands of state government bodies regulating utilities, labeled the Public Utilities Commission in West Virginia and the State Corporation Commission (SCC) in Virginia. Because some of the proposed routes of the power line crossed federal public land,

Radford University students Megan Scanlow and Shannon Scott visit with Ruth Reynolds on Ruth's front porch in Maywood/Simmonsville community of Sinking Creek Valley. Megan and Shannon are two of the participants studying "cultural attachment to place" under the direction of Melinda Wagner PhD, Professor of Anthropology, Radford University for Citizens for Preservation of Craig County. Ruth, a much beloved citizen of Craig County, on July 17th celebrated her 80th birthday. Practically all those years have been spent on Sinking Creek. Ruth says "if that power line's anywhere in Craig County, it's too close for me." Shannon commented "so many of the people we've talked with have that attitude. They appear to love all the county as if it was their backyard."

CPCC discusses alternatives
proposed by Forest Service

Two of Melinda Wagner's students researching "cultural attachment to place" interview an 80-year-old, lifetime resident of Craig County, Virginia. Clipping from *The New Castle Record*, New Castle, VA, 1994. (Courtesy of *The New Castle Record*)

an environmental impact assessment was required, with the U.S. Forest Service as the lead coordinating agency. Cultural attachment to land, along with many other aspects of the ecology and geology of the area, became a significant issue in this assessment.

Citizens who had served as resource persons for the Town Hall project requested an ethnographic study of cultural attachment to land in their county. The study we completed served as a supplement to the required environmental impact assessment. As we were called upon by other counties that lay in the path of various proposed routes for the power line, study of cultural attachment to land expanded to include eleven semesters, more than one hundred undergraduate students in four different courses, and 223 residents of five counties. It resulted in over four thousand pages of transcribed interviews ranging from twenty minutes to six hours in length, and over three thousand pages of computerized linguistic analyses of these data, along with some two thousand pages of thematic content analyses. It produced four technical reports, chapters and articles co-authored with students, an honors thesis, and numerous student and faculty presentations and performances on campus, for local historical societies, and at meetings of the Appalachian Studies Conference, the Southern Anthropological Society, and the American Anthropological Association, and expert witness testimony before the State Corporation Commission (Wagner 1999).

The motivation for beginning the cultural attachment to land studies is summarized in a statement by Setha Low (1994, 68): "Within the politics of place, poor people's neighborhoods are always the most vulnerable because the local constituency does not have the political and economic power to struggle against the definitions and decisions of governmental officials and private entrepreneurs." These definitions tend to be economic in idiom, and, as such, are at odds with understanding the complexities of cultures. Skip

Rappaport (1994, 265) wrote, "Under these circumstances essential public concerns which cannot be put into economic terms remain not only inaudible but even unarticulated."

We were also propelled by the fact that, according to the literature, ethnographic methods were becoming more accepted in social impact assessment (a part of environmental impact assessment) because of their ability to capture the natives' point of view. Colleagues like Benita Howell at the University of Tennessee contended that whereas a governmental regulatory commission might dismiss the emotional testimony of residents, carefully collected and analyzed ethnographic data might be attended to.

Eliot Liebow has asked, "Who ought to sit at the table when the big decisions get made? . . . Whose values should inform the choices?" (Liebow 1998/1999, 18). Following these questions, we determined that the objective of this project was to create ways in which citizens' environmental concerns such as cultural attachment to land could come to the table. Through rose-colored glasses we said, "It is a goal of this project to develop a method that is anthropologically sophisticated, informed by symbolic and political economy theories and by scientific positivist and humanistic interpretive approaches, yet that is at the same time practical for environmental impact assessment and community-based environmental protection efforts" (Wagner 1999, 2002, 2009). We sought a method that was nuanced yet practical.

Holding to the observation that resiliency is fostered by hearkening to narratives of downs as well as ups, some pitfalls will be discussed here. But as will be seen, they are the same pitfalls encountered in our research at large. For the most part, strategies for coping have already been developed.

I—Identity

This principle argues for the importance of keeping your Identity and paying attention to the identities of your community participants, and to their understandings of yours. As in traditional anthropological ethnographic fieldwork, the role we played was not always interpreted in the same way by us—anthropologist and anthropology students—and by our informants/collaborators/community partners. For example, I had told our major informant in a phone conversation that this kind of work was called cultural conservation. When the six student members of the first research team and I drove to his house to make entree and to become oriented to the county, he said, "I know you think you have a culture to conserve here, but we have a power line to stop" (Wagner and Hedrick 2001).

Again, how different is that from basic research? It is common for the ethnographer's role to be conceived somewhat differently by the ethnographer and by informants. A disjuncture in the understanding of the ethnographer's role requires exploring the differing perspectives with community partners, whether or not the research is "applied." An example from NSF-funded basic ethnographic research—applied only in the sense that a purpose of ethnography is to make the world safe for human differences, in Ruth Benedict's words—demonstrates the necessity to handle a similar issue in that milieu. The same issues occur and the same strategies work.

During research in conservative Christian schools during the late 1980s, scandals rocked the evangelical world. Collaborators in the Christian schools were concerned that my book would vilify them, as they thought journalists' reports were doing. Discussions of the methodology of anthropological data gathering ensued. They understood. They started pointing out *patterns* to me, in case I missed them. I explained that anthropology tries to capture the "natives'" point of view. One of the teachers said, "It's funny how you understand people better when you get to know them and understand why they do things" (Wagner 1983; 1990).

Building rapport and trust are a part of the methodology of basic and applied, international and local work. Undertaking the cultural attachment to land research, I was not fully aware of the distrust the local residents had for the colleges and universities in the area until I received this letter of thanks from Craig County resident Charles Spraker, handwritten on lined yellow paper: "We're all proud of you and your students for helping us open our eyes and see that what we know, feel, and are can be of value and is not useless . . . You know, Melinda, when we first started getting involved in this process . . . we were actually scared of our own colleges, as some of us thought they were looking down on us."

Ultimately, the cultural attachment to land research did yield rapport. The rapport gained between residents and university faculty and students fostered a nearly fictive kin relationship, and certainly a symbiotic one. Charles Spraker wrote: "We gained a lot from our involvement with you and your students and you all made us feel good about our station and way of life. So you, dear Melinda, learned from us and we learned from you, so in the end we're all winners."

We need look no further than the American Anthropological Association ethics statement for how to proceed when our identities and our collaborators' views of our roles seem to collide.[2] At the start of a long-term relationship with community partners who collect oral histories from local residents, the AAA Statement on Ethics: Principles of Professional Responsibility was circulated. The group members themselves adapted it for their purposes:

* * * * * * * * * * * * * * * * * * *

Floyd County Oral History Project
Adapted from the American Anthropological Association
Statement on Ethics

Principles of Professional Responsibility

1. PROTECT & HONOR
In research, anthropologists' first responsibility is to those they study. When there is conflict of interest, these individuals must come first. Anthropologists must do everything in their power to protect the physical, social, and psychological welfare and the honor, dignity, and privacy of those studied.

2. SAFEGUARD TRUST
Where research involves the acquisition of material and information transferred on the assumption of trust between persons, it is important that the rights, interests, and sensitivities of those studied must be safeguarded.

3. RESPECT ANONYMITY
Informants have a right to remain anonymous. This right should be respected both where it has been promised explicitly and where no clear understanding to the contrary has been reached. This applies to the collection of data by means of cameras, recorders, and other data-gathering devices, as well as to data collected in face-to-face interviews. But everyone should understand that anonymity may be compromised unintentionally.

4. FAIR IS FAIR
There should be no exploitation of individual informants for personal gain. Fair return should be given for all services.

5. THINK AHEAD
There is an obligation to reflect on the foreseeable repercussions of the study.

6. SHARE INTENTIONS
The anticipated consequences and likely forms of publication of research should be communicated as fully as possible to the individuals and groups likely to be affected.

7. MAKE FULL DISCLOSURE
Anthropologists should fully disclose the aims and sponsorship of research.

8. BE A GOOD GUEST
All work should be performed in full recognition of the social and cultural pluralism of host communities and the diversity of values, interests and demands in those societies.

* * * * * * * * * * * * * * * * * * *

B—Be willing to cross boundaries

In order to communicate successfully with community partners or the public at large, it is necessary to:

R—Reduce jargon; Relate; Communicate

One of my long-term community partners said while listening to students discuss Foucault, "Let's take these lofty ideas and put them on a hay bale." Notice that she did not say, "Let's take these lofty ideas and throw them into the cistern." She didn't want them to be thrown out. She wanted them to be communicated. Sabloff (2011) and later Moskowitz (2015) and others have noted a characteristic of anthropology that makes communicating to non-anthropologists problematic. "The basic anthropological story does not embrace a model of taking the extraordinary and making it ordinary, of making it relevant to people. Rather, we take the extraordinary and make it complicated" (Sabloff 2011, 413, quoting Daniel Linde's blog).

Engaged anthropology requires a commitment to communicate in forms useful to the community partners.

An engaged anthropology assumes a special responsibility to the communities of persons it studies. Rather than extracting knowledge from its social environment in pursuit of purely academic goals, knowledge developed within a community should be democratically produced, analyzed, and reported. This assumes our engaging the community in determining the goals of research and the methods by which it will be carried out. It also includes the community in the dissemination of research results that may involve nontraditional formats such as newsletters, forums, block meetings, or creative performances. Such democratization of knowledge does not preclude more traditional forms of academic discussion and reporting; nor does it diminish the anthropologist's potential role as interlocutor, speaking to powerful institutions outside the community. It does require the anthropologist to consider carefully the various audiences for anthropological research and appropriate strategies for communicating with them. (Blakey et al. 1994, 300)

Our foremothers traditionally wrote in ways that communicated with the public. Margaret Mead's editor, John Wiley, said of her, "She wrote as she spoke, very fluently and very fast. Clarity and sanity were her goals." If Margaret Mead were alive today, she would be a regular on the talk shows. Dr. Margaret would be as well-known as Dr. Phil. She would be asked for the anthropological perspective on all manner of things. And she would weigh in.

Now our students are carrying engaged anthropology to new heights. No one epitomizes cooperative collaboration with community partners at every stage of the research better than Eric Lassiter, co-author in this volume and who, I am proud to say, was my student as an undergraduate. Lassiter's award-winning collaborative ethnography represents the ultimate in community participation (Campbell and Lassiter 2010; Lassiter 2001a, 2001b, 2003, 2004, 2005a, 2005b, 2006, 2008, Lassiter and Campbell 2010a, 2010b; Lassiter et al. 2004; Papa and Lassiter 2003).

So as not to present an overly Pollyannaish view of the strains inherent in engaged anthropology, permit me to describe challenges that arose as the cultural attachment to land studies entered the high stakes power arena of the legal-like proceedings of the State Corporation Commission. In the new role of expert witness, I felt the heat of the grilling on the stand.

Students and I had been engaged in various projects—collecting oral histories for a county's museum, interviewing retired coal miners to learn about the place of religion in their lives for a Coal Mining Heritage Association—that were very satisfying to all concerned. These projects were also innocuous from a power point of view as there was no power establishment fighting back. The power line project upped the ante, pitting citizens against a corporation and the government body regulating it.

Our first research reports on cultural attachment to land had been given to citizens' groups to do with as they liked in their efforts to conserve their culture and preserve their environment. Then two adjoining counties requested that we present our report directly to the state regulatory body for utilities and testify in a hearing before this body. This brought us face-to-face with the legal arena and carried with it the new role of expert witness.

Stringent deadlines for citizen input were imposed by the State Corporation Commission and the very short timeline demanded some changes to the study design. It would not be possible for a cadre of trained students to compile extensive participant observation fieldnotes and to conduct and transcribe interviews, undertake analyses of these texts, and write the report, as we had done in the past. Citizens suggested that they themselves could conduct and transcribe the interviews.

This was a new level of citizen science. Previously residents with whom we worked had provided orientations for me and the student researchers and smoothed our entree into their communities; this time residents would be collecting data themselves. To help resident interviewers with data collecting, a comprehensive project manual compiled with my colleague Mary LaLone—which included open-ended questions that had been tested in my previous research—was developed, and workshops on ethnographic interviewing were conducted. If our experiment worked, perhaps it could serve as a model for allowing citizen input in the legal arena, especially for communities with little money or in situations with little time allowed.[3] My colored glasses became even rosier and I wrote, "The objective of this project is to create ways in which citizens' environmental concerns— such as cultural attachment to land—are rendered audible in a legal venue by being articulated through scientific means" (See Wagner 1999, 2002, Wagner and Hedrick 2001).

Both old and new trends in anthropology encouraged this new level of partnership. Collaboration has been advocated in anthropology since modern-day methods of fieldwork were formed; the trend is toward ever more collaboration. For example, the National Park Service in its Applied Ethnography Program headed by Muriel Crespi mandated collaboration with natives in learning about the relationship between culture and environment. Similarly, the Environmental Protection Agency's (EPA) Community-Based Environmental Protection program advocated citizen involvement and citizen data collecting.

We worked closely with the one attorney hired by the two counties to represent them at the State Corporation Committee hearing. In contrast, several attorneys and paralegal assistants from a large law firm worked on the side of the power company. Our attorney's background in engineering stood him in good stead with regard to understanding technical issues surrounding the power line. He was new to anthropology, but he learned quickly and became a strong advocate for ethnographic methods.

While we in the social sciences see this newborn interest in attending to the intangible aspects of culture in environmental impact assessments as a foot in the door, the corporations and utilities who are required to undertake the assessments see it as the camel's nose under the tent. And one way the camel will be kept outside is via the definition of science. Ethnography is seen as not scientific, whether it is or not. In the State Corporation Commission hearing examiner's report of the hearing, words implying expertise and science were applied only to certain activities and persons and not others. The six uses of the term "expert(s)" referred to those who studied real estate values, karst topography, and bats. Likewise, "research(er, ers)" referred to health, real estate values, and bats. All uses of "science" referred to studies of health-related issues. As the attorney for the protesting residents wrote in his "Exceptions to the Report," "the Report details the qualifications and professional experience of the witnesses supporting the Examiner's findings while failing to provide similar information for witnesses with opposing views."

As I took the stand in one of the sumptuously-appointed hearing rooms in the large State Corporation Commission building in the far-from-rural-counties state capital to defend ethnography in general, and our study of cultural attachment to land in particular, the weight of legal definitions pressed in. As folklorist Mary Hufford has said, there is a suspicion of storytelling and a separation of storytelling from science. Michael Orbach (2000) noted that policy managers use the stories of natural history—for example, the life history of a fish—and treat it as science, but stories about people are a different story. Although I have thought the often-quoted "Anthropology is the most scientific of the humanities, and the most humanistic of the sciences" captures anthropology's strength, it was clear that in this court-like atmosphere it was necessary for ethnography's image to be as scientific as possible. (The quote is probably Kroeber's, usually cited from Wolf 1964.)

One issue to raise its head was bias. For most of the hour and a half I was on the stand, the opposing attorney and I talked past one another concerning bias. Bear in mind that ours was not a study of attitudes toward the power line. Our study was an ethnography of particular aspects of culture with the guiding question, "Is there cultural attachment to land here, and if so on what is it based?" Thus, the only way the study could be biased, as far as we were concerned, was if it had been done in a way that demonstrated that cultural attachment to land was actually there when it wasn't, or vice versa. For the ethnographer, bias may arise in two ways. The first is that the researcher may hold unconscious points of view that prevent her from seeing certain things, or cause her to see only certain things at the expense of others that are equally present. Our methods avoided these pitfalls by using a standardized, although very open-ended, set of questions and by analyses that utilized a good deal of quantification. A second source of bias is that data could be collected in such a way that the interviewer might lead the interviewee to information, making it appear that the interviewee had more cultural knowledge than he or she actually had. Or the interviewer might interrupt the interviewee, not affording the opportunity to display cultural knowledge that was actually there. Again, our methods painstakingly controlled for this through an evaluation process that scrutinized the interviews before analyzing them. Thus, from our point of view, careful controls against bias had been an integral part of our methodology.

But for an attorney, bias is a different breed of cat, and the legal definition of bias can be used to endeavor to discredit. To avoid the appearance of bias in the legal sense, i.e. having a prejudice for or against one of the parties in the proceeding, I (and student researchers) had avoided becoming a member of or appearing at meetings of any of the protest groups or talking with the media. Nevertheless, the opposing lawyer's several specific questions culminated in this summary question, "Was this not power line opponents interviewing power line opponents for the purpose of opposing the power line? Is that not biased?"

Questions about the power line were not included in the set of questions to be asked. Because we were plumbing the culture of the area, the power line did come up in interviewees' discussions. That is not surprising. The interview transcriptions themselves were acquired by the opposing attorneys under a motion to compel discovery with which we complied after student researchers had carefully redacted all names. Opposing attorney staff members had diligently combed through the 449 pages and located three uses of the word power line. On the stand, I told them about seven more that they had missed, because to me this did not constitute bias. Instead, concern about the power line was an emerging part of the culture, and just one of several components of a larger cultural theme that the student researchers had discovered through coding and thematic analysis, namely "Protecting the Land." Other components of this theme included concern over trash being left on property and fences torn down, active county planning commissions, and resident-approved zoning regulations.

In the long run, the State Corporation Commission itself wrote: "The Commission disagrees with the Hearing Examiner's conclusions on bias in Ms. Wagner's study. We give weight to the study's conclusions that residents of the two counties . . . have individual and communal ties to particular pieces of land. We accept her conclusion that these residents have 'emotional, economic, and social connections to their surrounding landscapes.'"

The stories of the human community, in all their fullness and all their complexity, have to be told. It is worthwhile to strengthen the links between anthropological ethnographic research and local communities because "As soon as our attention turns from a community as a body of houses and tools and institutions to the states of mind of particular people, we are turning to the exploration of something immensely complex and difficult to know" (Redfield 1960, 59). The "BRIDGE" strategies noted above should allow us to Get Connected and Engage with local communities. If we are convinced that we have the methods and strategies to do engaged anthropology, how do local communities benefit?

Community Benefits

Sharing anthropological expertise with community members, nonprofit organizations, government agencies, or people who need help communicating with government agencies is empowering. At the State Corporation Commission decision-making table, the communities' voices were amplified because of the data collection and analysis that the cultural attachment to land project provided. A second source of empowerment was unanticipated. A by-product of the relationships we formed with the residents is that it raised awareness of cultural heritage. Linking with a university professor and students was empowering with regard to demonstrating to the culture-bearers that others valued and were interested in their cultures. It chipped away at the accretions built up by years of stereotyping of rural Appalachian people. When student researchers presented a play that they had created to the Craig County Historical Society, impersonating Craig County residents with words from the interviews, an audience member commented, "This has made me proud of my heritage," a feeling she had never before felt. The next day one of the students said, "I couldn't sleep at all last night; I was so wound up after that reception we got." Local historian Nancy Kate Givens said that letting families know about the results of the research was pleasurable. "They knew they had been here forever, but no one had presented that as something to brag about" (Link, Brady, and Givens 2002, 150). This same thought is captured by Supreme Court Justice Sonia Sotomayor (2013, 149) when she wrote in her autobiography, "Every people has a past, but the dignity of a history comes when a community of scholars devotes itself to chronicling and studying that past."

Citizen involvement in the research—that is, collaboration—was critical to empowerment. Native-born Giles County resident, Doris Lucas Link, wrote, "When I became involved in the AEP fight in 1993, I never imagined it would take me to college [to teach my classes about her community], make an amateur architect of me, send me to the state capitol to speak before the [State Corporation Commission], . . . [and cause me to speak] at an Appalachian Studies Conference" (Link, Brady, and Givens 2002, 138-39).

Community voices at the table will be fortified by professional work obtained within their means and within a symbiotic relationship. As mentioned earlier, engaged anthropology comes in many forms. Description of a project undertaken for several years by my colleague, Mary LaLone, provides an example of a different type of project with some of the same and some different benefits. Dr. LaLone and her students, in partnership with a grassroots community group and local government offices, rescued the coal mining heritage of Montgomery County, Virginia, that was in danger of being forgotten. Mary's first project was the New River Valley Coal Mining Heritage project. Working with the Coal Mining Heritage

Association, students collected elders' oral histories and compiled them into a set of books: *Appalachian Coal Mining Memories* and *Coal Mining Lives.* These two volumes contain sixty-one interviews with forty-three men and thirty women, describing their lives as coal miners, miners' wives, and miners' children. The community partners expanded to include the county planning office when the oral history project led to the Coal Mining Heritage Park project. LaLone and her students wrote a 136-page consulting report: *Coal Mining Heritage Park: Study, Plans, and Recommendations* (LaLone 1997, 1998, 1999, 2001, 2003, 2005, 2009).

Mary LaLone's Radford University students interview
former miner Fred Lawson describing mining tools.
(Photo courtesy of Mary LaLone)

In 2005, the Appalachian Studies Association conference was held at Radford University, with the theme *University Community Partnerships.* The plenary session celebrated several of these partnerships from the New River Valley of Virginia, including Mary

LaLone's projects. Jimmy Lee Price, a community partner in the Coal Mining Heritage projects, spoke at the 2005 plenary session, describing how the projects had benefited the community.

> We wanted and needed to create a coal mining heritage park that could combine history, education, science, and recreation, and promote the health along the Huckleberry Trail—and so it was a big job and we didn't have the expertise to do it, didn't have the training, didn't have much of the technical support that we needed. Besides it would have cost us hundreds of thousands of dollars to hire consultants and engineers. I've estimated that the university saved us approximately a quarter of a million dollars in consulting and engineering fees. Not to mention the cultural and social benefits to all the partners . . . And so, what we received from this partnership, I'll just enumerate a few things. As I said, probably a quarter of a million dollars in consulting and design costs free of charge. Human resources—unbelievable and gratifying to work with.
>
> One of the things we did was to invite the students to our monthly meetings and fed them good home cooked meals and then we learned to sing each others' songs. I've kind of used that as a bridge, as a cultural bridge, and it occurred to me one night, well we're so different, from different environments, what do we have in common? And I thought "Hey, we can all sing Amazing Grace." And so we did—and we learned essentially to sing each others' songs and to speak each others' languages.
>
> And so we gained a crucial influence of major university involvement. This element built our own power and influence in dealing with government officials, the press, and other institutions. Or, I'll say it this way, it was a creation of a larger community of actors. And so it just sort

of doubled or increased our power to do what we needed to do. (Price 2005)

If we are convinced that we possess strategies for doing engaged anthropology locally, do we have strategies for being *allowed* to do engaged anthropology locally?

Strategies for Being Allowed to Do Anthropology to Benefit Local Communities (How to Fit it into Your Professional Life and Career and Get Credit for it)

In an alternative culture that we could easily create in our minds, the default would be locally engaged anthropology. It would not be something that needs defense. What if the word "local" were as celebrated as the word "global"? What if universities were as concerned about localizing their curricula as they are globalizing and internationalizing them? But they are not. So, alas, engaging locally requires defense. Where does that defense come from?

Professional Labels

"Engaged anthropology" has come to be the umbrella term for a wide range of activities. Kozaitis (2013) notes that "Anthropologists in the United States have named the production and application of empirical knowledge to help meet human needs and solve social problems as applied, action, practicing, professional, militant, activist, engaged, public, advocacy, public interest, and praxis anthropology" (Kozaitis 2013, 137).

Professional labels that are used across disciplines include "Participatory Action Research" (PAR), "Participatory Development," and "Social Capital." Eliot Liebow's (1998/1999, 18) quote mentioned earlier captures the essence of participatory development: "Who ought to sit at the table when the big decisions get made? . . . Whose values should inform the choices?"

I must register a bit of discomfort when using terms such as "stakeholders" and "social capital." I have decried the overwhelming place economy has in our society when set beside concerns for environment and sense of place. Yet we in social science are now using economically-derived terms to describe ways to help communities voice their concerns and to balance economic needs with other cultural values. Nevertheless, the vocabulary of social capital may help to describe some of the ways engaged anthropology can proceed.

A broad definition of social capital is "the connections among individuals—social networks and the norms of reciprocity and trustworthiness that arise from them." The terms that define different kinds of social capital—bonding, bridging, and linking—refer to which groups are connecting (Furbey et al. 2006; see also Woolcock 2001 and Gilchrist 2004). For example, linking social capital forms relationships "between people or organizations beyond peer boundaries, cutting across status, and similarity, and enabling people to exert influence and reach resources outside their normal circles" (Furbey et al. 2006, 7). Social capital as it played out in the power line projects helped to make a place at the table for local communities. Resident David Brady wrote, "These studies helped the community . . . articulate the issue of attachment [to land] to decision-makers at the state and federal level" (Link, Brady, and Givens 2002, 145; Wagner 2009).

These professional labels may buttress the recognition of engaged anthropology at the university level and the individual career level. Senior faculty have a special responsibility in fostering this recognition. Those who sit on department, college, and university personnel committees that frame the standards for tenure and promotion have a duty to work to broaden the scope of valued activities to include engaged work. Define this work as professional and as professionally important. Assure junior faculty that if they engage in this kind of work, it will not be seen as a shortcoming on their Faculty Annual Reports and it will not be a detriment when decisions are made about the future of their careers. I am not the first, nor will I be the last, to say this. The American Anthropological Association panel's Statement to the Profession in *Diagnosing America* notes, "Anthropologists have become increasingly submerged in a professional ethic that rewards the development of abstract theory over practice, encourages individual attainment over collaboration, and places a premium on arcane debate over engagement with broader publics and pressing social issues" (Blakey et al. 1994, 297). Jeremy Sabloff, in his Distinguished Lecture at the 2010 American Anthropological Association, made the point that the trend in counting numbers of peer-reviewed articles—rather than a more qualitative evaluation that would take into account the significance of public anthropology work—needs to be reversed. He invokes former AAA president James Peacock's shibboleth that we need a "public or perish" stance (Peacock 1997; Sabloff 2010). In 2008, the Consortium of Practicing and Applied Anthropology (COPAA) published a 12-page document on "Promoting Applied Scholarship for Tenure and Promotion," and COPAA regularly discusses these issues at their annual meetings (Kahnna et al. 2008; see also Bennett and Kahnna 2010).

If junior faculty discover that a research report, or analysis report, or other item useful to their community partners is not enough for their personnel committees, they could consider publishing their results in organs dedicated to community or regional work or to the pedagogical benefits of the work. Another strategy which can be both practical and satisfying is to connect with area studies: Appalachian Studies, American Studies, Women's Studies. Connections can open new arenas for research, for collaboration with colleagues, and for venues in which to present research. Making these connections formed one of the recommendations of the American

Anthropological Association's panel on Disorders of Industrial Societies.

Whiteford and Strom (2013) note that "service" activities, though required for faculty, are undervalued in tenure and promotion protocols. Sabloff (2011) noted that teaching is also often undervalued. But separating teaching from professional work from service to the community is old news. Ever since Ernest Boyer's vision was published as *The Scholarship of Engagement* in 1996, connecting the three—teaching, research, and service—has been an honorable thing to do. "The scholarship of engagement means connecting the rich resources of the university to our most pressing social, civic and ethical problems."

Accreditation, which may sometimes seem to contribute little to the goal of student-learning, can, nevertheless be used to move the concern for the local forward. For example, for the last several five-year accreditation cycles, schools accredited by the Southern Association of Colleges and Schools (SACS) have been required to develop a Quality Enhancement Plan (QEP). The current QEP for Radford University is the Scholar-Citizen Initiative (SCI) which dovetails with collaborative work with local communities.[4]

Pedagogical Labels and Pedagogical Benefits

Evolving pedagogical labels demonstrate an interest in activities that convey students beyond the classroom. In evolutionary chart form (oldest at the bottom), some of them are:

> Engaged Pedagogy
> High Impact Practices
> Student Engagement
> Transformative/Transformational Learning
> Scholar-Citizen
> Experiential Learning
> Service Learning

What are the pedagogical benefits for the undergraduate and graduate students who participate in these research and service endeavors? Kozaitis (2013, 150) notes that "public engagement by university faculty and students . . . requires empirical data, intellectual rigor, political responsibility, critical sociocultural analysis, and theoretically informed strategies and methods of partnered reforms that reinforce social justice."

The projects described here worked as pedagogical tools to cause undergraduate students to do extraordinary work and to dispel stereotypes of Appalachian mountain people they may have carried into the classroom with them. There were several reasons they were motivating to students. For example:

1. The final products had an audience beyond the teacher.

2. Sometimes grants and contracts were received, symbolizing the worth of the students' work to outside audiences.

3. The students were dealing with real people, and sometimes the real people have real problems. Student Danny Wolfe, speaking of the power line Town Meeting project, said, "The fact that we were dealing with real people and a topic that we could relate to was the key to making it a success. We tried to put ourselves into these people's shoes . . . Before the project and fieldwork were done, we felt a part of their lives and the wiser for having taken on this task."

4. Students and teacher worked together as research colleagues, creating a community of learners. Student Shannon Scott said, "This project was not done in a normal classroom setting where we were told what needed to be done. Instead we were all able to work together—students and professor—in a democratic way. Everyone's input was taken into consideration. Never did we feel like what we had to say was unimportant . . . My self-esteem was raised, because my professor trusted me to do this work."

For undergraduate and graduate students, projects of engaged anthropology with communities allow a view into sophisticated anthropological work, and can open avenues to explore after graduation. Shannon Scott said that the cultural attachment to land project

> . . . not only gave undergraduates a project to put on their resumes, but it also gave them the opportunity to get out into the field and experience what doing anthropology is really about. By getting involved in this project, students were given the opportunity to work in an atmosphere where what we did would really matter . . . For many of us this was not a project for a grade but a project that allowed us to work one-on-one with our professor and gain the knowledge and self-esteem that will be needed when we move out of undergraduate school into either a career or graduate school. (Wagner, Scott, and Wolfe 1997)

Gary Cutlip, then Bland County administrator, wrote a letter to each undergraduate student researcher, in which he said, "Those who have seen the study are most impressed with your work . . . You provided us with a document that will prove to be invaluable to the county in many ways . . . We wish you much luck in your future endeavors as an anthropologist. May your enthusiasm continue to provide you with challenges that will make differences in the future of our country."

At the *University Community Partnerships* plenary session of the 2005 Appalachian Studies Association, Mary LaLone's student, Stacy Spradlin Haynes, spoke about what the Coal Mining Heritage projects had meant to her as a student. Her speech that day revealed another reward for students. Practicing anthropological skills enhances the depth of observations of lives lived, including one's own.

In one short semester, we were taught how to interview, how to transcribe, and how to edit these interviews—but that's definitely not all that we learned. We also learned that college does not have to be a time for us, as students, to only be on the receiving end. While at college, through partnerships like this, we can actually give back to the community around our school. I was only eighteen at the time of this class and here I was being asked to sit down with people who were in their sixties, seventies, eighties, and even nineties, and have a two hour or longer conversation with them about their lives . . . And I also thought that growing up in a coal mining community, I knew all the stories that had been told about the area. I thought I knew exactly everything that was going to be said—but boy did I have a lot to learn!

It wasn't until I sat down with my great-grandmother who was ninety-six years old at the time that I began to actually feel these stories that I had heard all of my life. That day I listened to great-grandmother tell about when she was fifteen years old and she jumped the Huckleberry Train with my great-grandpa and ran off to Tennessee to get married. Now granted, I'd heard that story umpteen million times, but that day as I sat down with her, I saw the longing in her eyes for her sweetheart who'd passed away years before I was even born. I heard the hesitation in her voice as she described what it was like to come back home to her daddy, who to say the least was not very happy with them for running away. I saw the tears stream down her face as she described the ups and the downs of raising thirteen children on a miner's income. That day, I felt her unwavering faith in God that spanned her entire life. I realized the burden that she carried all those years—the burden of whether that day, tomorrow, or next week, she would be made a widow and her children would have to grow up without a daddy.

Today, as a wife and a mother, those words that my great-grandmother spoke to me bring comfort to my own soul as I undertake the task of raising my own children . . . As I began to feel these stories that I'd heard my entire life, I realized the weight that all of us can carry on our own shoulders—the weight of our own heritage. While some may carry theirs lightly, I made the decision to carry mine with boldness, with honor, and to do all that I can to preserve this heritage. (Haynes 2005)

Just as Mary LaLone's student observed the rebound to her own life of her foray into ethnographic research, so too Adams and London and Klaaren in this volume describe the multiplex learning that occurs. An oft-repeated quote from Margaret Mead says, "Never doubt that a small group of thoughtful, committed citizens can change the world. Indeed, it is the only thing that ever has." I have wondered whether Margaret Mead would have taught Anthropology in high school. I don't know if she would. (She did write a book about anthropology for high school students.) But I would. And I do. Community partners at the Floyd Story Center, a nonprofit organization, Floyd County High School, and Radford University are in our tenth year of *Roots with Wings: Floyd County Place-based Education Oral History Project*. Radford University mentors work as part of an intergenerational team to teach high school students how to conduct ethical, methodologically sound interviews; record using state-of-the-art audio and video equipment; transcribe; create searchable tables of content; research historical background; archive; extract a theme from hour-long interviews; and create movies. The overall goal of the project is to make connections among the multi-aged participants: high school students, university student mentors who teach ethnographic research skills, adult community partners, high school teachers, university faculty, and elder interviewees. Youth taught to capture the wisdom of elders learn lessons of past hardships and absorb demonstrations of coping skills. Research has shown that connections like these propagate children who are more resilient in the face of challenges such as negative stereotyping, community and family dysfunction, or culture change, because they have a "strong intergenerational self."

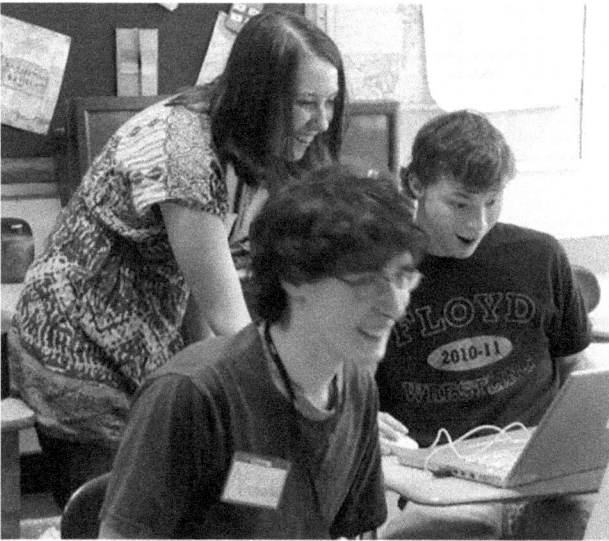

Radford University ROOTS WITH WINGS
student mentor shares movie-making expertise
with Floyd County High School students.
(Photo courtesy of Melinda Bollar Wagner)

It is worthwhile and necessary to develop the links between anthropological ethnographic research and local communities because the stories of the human community—as full, rich, complex, and intricate as they are—have to be told. Eric Lassiter (1999, 7) wrote in the *Anthropology Newsletter*: "The more we extend our conversations to include those traditionally outside anthropological discourse, the more we can foster our unique perspectives as anthropologists. Making ethnography relevant to our consultants—who are increasingly becoming our readers—is more than a methodological or theoretical move, it is also an ethical act." It's the right thing to do. Go into the grandest building on your campus grounds. Look around. Look up at the chandeliers. Look at the walnut paneling. Look at the terrazzo floors. Ask yourself—why is this here? What should we be doing as a university situated within this place—this place with real people with real problems and with real perceptions and understandings.

APPENDIX:

COMMUNITY-BASED PROJECTS LED BY MELINDA BOLLAR
WAGNER, 1983-2017

In chronological order:
- The ABC's of Appalachia and Beyond the ABC's of Appalachia
- Appalachia: A Tourist Attraction?
- Mileposts and More: The Blue Ridge Parkway
- Crossings: Into Twentieth Century Appalachia
- V-QUEST (Virginia Quality Education in Science and Technology) Learning about Teaching
- Cultural Attachment to Land in Proposed 765kV Power Line Corridors
- Spiritual and Cultural Significance of Mountains in National Parks, Exhibit at Great Smoky Mountains National Park Headquarters
- Religion in the Coal Mines
- Floyd County Traditions
- Little River in Floyd County, Project for the New River Land Trust
- Appalachian Studies Conference at RU, 2005, Showcasing University-Community Partnerships
- Mountain View Cemetery
- Floyd County Migration
- Religion and Health in an Appalachian Community Project
- Appalachian Social Movement Project
- Appalachian Regional Commission Appalachian Teaching Project: Sustaining the Community Mind for Long-term Community Resiliency: Rural Appalachian Values Assessment in Floyd County, Virginia, Project for the Floyd County Community and Economic Development Office
- ROOTS WITH WINGS: Floyd County Place-based Education Oral History Project

NOTES

1. See Goldschmidt 1976 and Schensul 2010 for a discussion of this history; Low and Merry 2010 provide an update on the history of engaged anthropology.
2. See also Checker, Davis, and Schuller 2014 for discussion of competing expectations. See Johnston 2010 for a discussion of ethics. See Moskowitz 2015 for a less optimistic view of synchrony between academic and applied anthropology.
3. A model for participatory research/citizen science was the Appalachian Land Ownership Study conducted in 1978-1981 by the Appalachian Alliance and administered by Appalachian State University and the Highlander Research and Education Center.
4. See *https://www.radford.edu/content/scholar-citizen/home.html*.

WORKS CITED

Bennett, Linda A. and Sunil K. Khanna. 2010. "A Review of Tenure and Promotion Guidelines in Higher Education: Optimistic Signs for Applied, Practicing, and Public Interest Anthropology." *American Anthropologist* 112 (4): 648-50.

Bennett, Linda A. and Linda M. Whiteford. 2013. "Anthropology and the Engaged University: New Vision for the Discipline within Higher Education." *Annals of Anthropological Practice* 37 (1): 2-18.

Blakey, Michael L., Frank Dubinskas, Shepard Forman, Carol MacLennan, Katherine S. Newman, James L. Peacock, Roy A. Rappaport, Carlos G. Velez-Ibanez, and Alvin W. Wolfe. 1994. "A Statement to the Profession: The American Anthropological Association, Panel on Disorders of Industrial Societies." In *Diagnosing America: Anthropology and Public Engagement*, edited by Shepard Forman, 295-312. Ann Arbor: University of Michigan Press.

Boyer, Ernest L. 1996. "The Scholarship of Engagement." *Bulletin of the American Academy of Arts and Sciences* 49 (7): 18-33.

Campbell, Elizabeth and Luke Eric Lassiter. 2010. "From Collaborative Ethnography to Collaborative Pedagogy: Reflections on the Other Side of Middletown Project and Community-University Research Partnerships." *Anthropology & Education Quarterly* 41 (4): 370-85.

Checker, Melissa. 2014. "Anthropological Superheroes and the Consequences of Activist Ethnography." *American Anthropologist* 116 (2): 416-20.

Checker, Melissa, Dana-Ain Davis, and Mark Schuller. 2014. "The Conflicts of Crisis: Critical Reflections on Feminist Ethnography and Anthropological Activism." *American Anthropologist* 116 (2): 408-20.

Forman, Shepard, ed. 1994. *Diagnosing America: Anthropology and Public Engagement*, Ann Arbor: University of Michigan Press.

Furbey, Robert, Adam Dinham, Richard Farnell, Doreen Finneron, and Guy Wilkinson. 2006. *Faith as Social Capital: Connecting or Dividing?* Bristol, UK: The Policy Press.

Gilchrist, Alison. 2004. *The Well-Connected Community: A Networking Approach to Community Development*. Bristol, UK: The Policy Press.

Goldschmidt, Walter. 1976. "Anthropology and America." *Social Science Quarterly* 57 (1): 154-81.

Gordan, Joan. 1976. *Margaret Mead: The Complete Bibliography, 1925–1975*. The Hague: Mouton.

Haynes, Stacy Spradlin. 2005. "University Community Partnerships Plenary Session." Paper presented at the Appalachian Studies Conference, Radford University, Radford, VA, March 19.

Hyland, Stanley E. and Linda A. Bennett. 2013. "Responding to Community Needs Through Linking Academic and Practicing Anthropology: An Engaged Scholarly Framework." *Annals of Anthropological Practice* 37 (1): 34-56.

Hyland, Stanley E. and Kristen Maurette. 2010. "Developing Poverty Reform in the Memphis Region: Lessons for an Engaged Anthropology." *Urban Anthropology and Studies of Cultural Systems and World Economic Development* 39 (3): 213-64.

Johnston, Barbara Rose. 2010. "Social Responsibility and the Anthropological Citizen." *Current Anthropology* 51 (2): 235-47.

Khanna, Sunil K., Nancy Romero-Daza, Sherylyn Briller, and Linda A. Bennett. 2008. "Promoting Applied Scholarship for Tenure & Promotion." Consortium of Practicing and Applied Anthropology Programs (COPAA). https://copaainfo.files.wordpress.com/2015/10/tenure-and-promotion-for-applied-anthropologists.pdf

Kozaitis, Kathryn A. 2013. "Anthropological Praxis in Higher Education." *Annals of Anthropological Practice* 37 (1): 133-55.

LaLone, Mary 1997. *Appalachian Coal Mining Memories: Life in Virginia's New River Valley Coal Fields*. Blacksburg, VA.: Pocahontas Press.

———. 1998. *Coal Mining Lives: An Oral History Sequel to Appalachian Coal Mining Memories*. Radford, VA.: Radford University Department of Sociology and Anthropology.

———. 1999. "Preserving Appalachian Heritage: A Model for Oral History Research and Teaching." *Journal of Appalachian Studies* 5 (1): 115-22.

———. 2001. "Putting Anthropology to Work to Preserve Appalachian Heritage." *Practicing Anthropology* 23 (2): 5-9.

———. 2003. "Walking the Line between Alternative Interpretations in Heritage Education and Tourism: A Demonstration of the Complexities with an Appalachian Coal Mining Example." In *Signifying Serpents & Mardi Gras Runners: Representing Identity in Selected Souths*, edited by Celeste Ray and Luke Eric Lassiter, 72-92. Athens: University of Georgia Press.

———. 2005. "Building Heritage Partnerships: Working Together for Heritage Preservation and Local Tourism in Appalachia. *Practicing Anthropology* 27 (4): 10-13.

———. 2009 "Guidelines for a Partnership Approach to Appalachian Community and Heritage Preservation Work." In *Participatory Development in Appalachia: Cultural Identity, Community, and Sustainability*, edited by Susan E. Keefe, 201-29. Knoxville: University of Tennessee Press.

Lassiter, Luke Eric. 1999. "We Keep What We Have by Giving it Away." *Anthropology News* 40 (1): 3, 7.

———. 2001a. "Engaging a Localized Public Anthropology." *Anthropology News* 42 (2): 7-8.

———. 2001b. "From 'Reading Over the Shoulders of Natives' to 'Reading Alongside Natives,' Literally: Toward a Collaborative and Reciprocal Ethnography." *Journal of Anthropological Research* 57 (2): 137-49.

———. 2003. "Theorizing the Local." *Anthropology News* 44 (5): 13.

———. 2004. "Collaborative Ethnography." *AnthroNotes* 25 (1): 1-14.

———. 2005a. "Collaborative Ethnography and Public Anthropology." *Current Anthropology* 46 (1): 83-106.

———. 2005b. *The Chicago Guide to Collaborative Ethnography.* Chicago: University of Chicago Press.

———. 2006. "Collaborative Ethnography Matters." *Anthropology News* 47 (5): 20-21.

———. 2008. "Moving Past Public Anthropology and Doing Collaborative Research." *National Association of Practicing Anthropologists, Bulletin* 29: 70-86. Washington, D.C.: American Anthropological Association.

Lassiter, Luke Eric and Elizabeth Campbell. 2010a. "Serious Fieldwork: On Re-functioning Ethnographic Pedagogies." *Anthropology News* 51 (6): 4, 8.

——— 2010b. "What Will We Have Ethnography Do?" *Qualitative Inquiry* 16 (9): 757-67.

Lassiter, Luke Eric, Hurley Goodall, Elizabeth Campbell, and Michelle Na-
tasya Johnson. 2004. *The Other Side of Middletown: Exploring Muncie's
African American Community.* New York: AltaMira Press.

Liebow, Edward B. 1998/1999. "The Heart of the Problem: The Local
Burden of National Policies." *Common Ground: Archaeology and Eth-
nography in the Public Interest,* double issue: Stewards of the Human
Landscape.

Link, Doris Lucas, David Brady, and Nancy Kate Givens. 2002. "Defend-
ing the Community: Citizen Involvement in Impact Assessment and
Cultural Heritage Conservation." In *Culture, Environment, and Conservation in the Appalachian South,* edited by Benita J. Howell, 137-52.
Urbana: University of Illinois Press.

Low, Setha M. 1994. "Cultural Conservation of Place." In *Conserving Culture: A New Discourse on Heritage,* edited by Mary Hufford, 66-77. Urbana: University of Illinois Press.

Low, Setha M. and Sally Engle Merry. 2010. "Engaged Anthropology: Diversity and Dilemmas." *Current Anthropology* 51 (2): 203-26.

Moskowitz, Nona. 2015. "Engagement, Alienation, and Anthropology's
New Moral Dilemmas." *Anthropology and Humanism* 40 (1): 35-57.

Norris-Tirrell, Dorothy, Katherine Lambert-Pennington, and Stan Hyland.
2010. "Embedding Service Learning in Engaged Scholarship at Research Institutions to Revitalize Metropolitan Neighborhoods." *Journal of Community Practice* 18: 171-89.

Orbach, Michael K. 2000. "Anthropology and Marine Environmental Policy." Paper and discussion presented at the American Anthropological
Association, San Francisco, CA, November 15-19.

Papa, Lee and Luke Eric Lassiter. 2003. "The Muncie Race Riots of 1967,
Representing Community Memory through Public Performance, and
Collaborative Ethnography between Faculty, Students and the Local
Community." *Journal of Contemporary Ethnography* 32 (2): 147-66.

Peacock, James L. 1997. "The Future of Anthropology." *American Anthropologist* 99 (1): 9-17.

Price, Jimmie Lee. 2005. "University Community Partnerships Plenary
Session." Paper presented at the Appalachian Studies Conference, Radford University, Radford, VA, March 19.

Rappaport, Roy A. 1994. "Disorders of Our Own: A Conclusion." In *Diagnosing America: Anthropology and Public Engagement*, edited by Shepard Forman, 235-94. Ann Arbor: University of Michigan Press.

Redfield, Robert. 1960. *The Little Community: Peasant Society and Culture.* Chicago: University of Chicago Press. (1973 printing)

Sabloff, Jeremy A. 2011 "Where Have You Gone, Margaret Mead? Anthropology and Public Intellectuals." *American Anthropologist* 113 (3): 408-416.

Schensul, Jean J. 2010. "Engaged Universities, Community Based Research Organizations and Third Sector Science in a Global System." *Human Organization* 69 (4): 307-20.

Sotomayor, Sonia. 2013. *My Beloved World.* New York: Alfred A. Knopf.

Wagner, Melinda Bollar. 1983. *Metaphysics in Midwestern America.* Columbus: Ohio State University Press.

———. 1990. *God's Schools: Choice and Compromise in American Society.* New Brunswick, NJ: Rutgers University Press.

———. 1999. "Measuring Cultural Attachment to Place in a Proposed Power Line Corridor." *Journal of Appalachian Studies* 5 (2): 241-46.

———. 2002. "Space and Place, Land and Legacy." In *Culture, Environment, and Conservation in the Appalachian South*, edited by Benita J. Howell, 121-32. Urbana: University of Illinois Press.

———. 2009. "Playing the Power Game: The Limits of Participatory Development." In *Participatory Development in Appalachian Communities: Essays on Cultural Identity, Social Capital and Sustainability*, edited by Susan E. Keefe, 141-56. Knoxville: University of Tennessee Press.

Wagner, Melinda Bollar and Kristen L. Hedrick. 2001. "'You Have a Culture to Preserve Here, But We Have a Power Line to Stop': University/Community Study of Cultural Attachment to Place." *Practicing Anthropology* 23 (2): 10-14.

Wagner, Melinda Bollar, Shannon T. Scott, and Danny Wolfe. 1997. "Drawing the Line Between People and Power: Taking the Classroom to the Community." In *Practicing Anthropology in the South*, edited by James M. Wallace, 109-18. Athens, GA: University of Georgia Press.

Wali, Alaka, Melissa Checker, and David Vine. 2010. "Introducing Public Anthropology Reviews." *American Anthropologist* 112 (4): 638-50.

Whiteford, Linda and Elizabeth Strom. 2013. "Building Community Engagement and Public Scholarship into the University." *Annals of Anthropological Practice* 37 (1): 72-89.

Wolf, Eric R. 1964. *Anthropology.* Englewood Cliffs, NJ: Prentice-Hall.

Woolcock, M. 2001. "The Place of Social Capital in Understanding Social and Economic Outcomes," *Isuma: Canadian Journal of Policy Research* 2 (1): 1-17.

Doing Ethnography to Connect, Exchange, and Impact

Brian A. Hoey

Connecting: What is Ethnography?

The term ethnography has come to be equated with virtually any qualitative research project where the intent is to provide a detailed, in-depth description of everyday life and practice. This wide claim of "ethnography" as a label to categorize all such research may, in fact, be too liberal in its application. Within the field of anthropology, an attempt to authentically render culturally-informed lived experience in written account is often referred to as "thick description," a term generally attributed to the anthropologist Clifford Geertz (1973) writing on what he described as an interpretive theory of culture in the early 1970s.[1] The term "ethnography," in fact, is meant to convey how this methodology unavoidably entails the act of rendering—in all senses of that evocative word—varied cultural lives into the written word.[2] As suggested by Renée Fox (2004, 311), I tend to reserve the term *ethnography* for qualitative research that involves some manner of "prolonged immersion in the field and continuous, face-to-face interaction with informants [. . .] that results in the generation of massive amounts of 'thickly descriptive' data, in a potentially narrative form, that provide an intimate view of what is being studied . . . [and to] distinguish it from *non-ethnographic* qualitative research that employs observation and interviewing methods in more circumscribed, short-term, distant, and 'thin' ways."

Use of the term "qualitative," as above, is typically meant to distinguish this kind of social science research from those projects considered "quantitative" in nature. As we might expect, the *quantitative* label suggests research more fully dependent on numbers such as statistically-driven approaches to data collection and analysis. Within such research, numeric data allows for comparatively rapid collection from much larger samples (the individuals and/or groups in a given study) as well as swifter analysis and representation of data than would be practically possible (or even desirable) within ethnographic fieldwork, especially ethnographic fieldwork that is truly "thick" in its description. Quantitative and the qualitative approaches, while potentially complimentary in usage, have a broad range of differences that I will not be discussing.

While an ethnographic approach to social research is no longer exclusively that of the cultural anthropologist, I tend to seek an understanding rooted in ethnography's disciplinary home. Anthropologists typically speak of ethnography as a particular qualitative research *process* (one conducts an ethnography) as well as a *product* (the written outcome is an ethnography), the aim of which is cultural interpretation. The ethnographer goes beyond simply reporting events and details of experience as we might, perhaps too simplistically, expect in the somewhat more (and deliberately) circumscribed role of a documentarian. Specifically, he or she attempts to explain how various observed and derived details of fieldwork represent what we might call "webs of significance," as was famously suggested by Geertz (1973, 5) in his phrasing for the complex, interconnected, and historically contingent cultural constructions in which we all live our lives.

Ethnographers endeavor to generate understandings of culture through depictions of what we may call an *emic* perspective, or what is often described as an "insider's point of view." The emphasis in this representation is on allowing critical categories and meanings to *emerge* from the ethnographic encounter rather than imposing these from pre-existing models. An *etic* perspective, by contrast, refers to a more distant, analytical orientation to the experience of fieldwork research. The linguist and anthropologist Kenneth Pike (1954, 8) devised these concepts by drawing on the linguistic terms of "phonemic" and "phonetic," respectively. In so doing, he suggested an original focus on the meaning of sounds within a given linguistic and cultural milieu or system in the *emic* perspective and a focus on universal functionality of sounds, without reference to embedded meaning, in the *etic* perspective. Pike initially described how an *emic* approach was an attempt to discover and describe particular linguistic patterns in terms of the broader context of a given language or culture as encountered directly in the field. This is in contrast to a primary concern for generalizable statements about such data in an *etic* approach. Such generalizable statements are intended to provide truly broad (i.e., global) classification and, importantly as we shall see below, *comparison* to a system of knowledge created prior to the particular fieldwork encounter. Following this distinction between *etic* and *emic,* an ethnographic understanding is developed through close exploration of a variety of sources of and approaches to data, while always relying on a cultural frame of analysis and interpretation.

In considering Pike's notable contribution to ethnographic vernacular and practice, we are introduced to what may well be an inevitable and, for many, necessary component of that practice. Anthropology is commonly described to undergraduate students in introductory textbooks as being fundamentally comparative in nature. Specifically, cultural anthropology is often defined as consisting of the fieldwork methodology of ethnography operationally paired with the analytical and theoretical work enabled by cross-cultural comparison of ethnographically-derived data on specific cultural groups—termed "ethnology" by many authors. For those who adopt this particular understanding of the conduct of cultural anthropology, comparison is an explicit component, at least in its future application, of the conduct of ethnography and of the representation of the findings of fieldwork research in ethnographic literature. That is to say, the work necessarily entails the identification and some manner of reification of what are taken to be meaningful social, cultural, and conceptual categories (derived from the local) with the purpose of establishing the strategic grounds on which we will speak, as anthropologists, of "similarities" and "differences" between human groups and, in so doing, come to some better appreciation of what it means to be human. An appreciation of what some, in fact, might refer to as the "human condition."

There is a persistent and widely-shared understanding that this is how the field is and should, generally, be portrayed, as well as an extensive history of purposeful comparisons in the literature of the discipline that are at times employed to create what are now long discredited rankings of "cultures" as well as relativistic comparisons of observed cultural patterns. However, the use of such explicit comparison between what are taken to be distinct cultural groups has for some time lost its appeal for many card-carrying anthropologists following the post-structuralist period of the 1970s and '80s. Nevertheless, comparison arguably remains an inalienable part of the work of ethnography, even if the subjects and objects being compared have shifted and the comparison may now serve different purposes. For much contemporary ethnography, my own included, comparison today incorporates what may be either an implicit or explicit dependence on the embodied subject-position of the ethnographer him or herself that corresponds with his or her particular cultural knowledge and point of view in what may be understood (if not exactly depicted) as an unavoidable (and, yes, comparative) place from which our research must begin. At the same time—in a manner further relevant given the particular theme of the volume to which this chapter contributes—much ethnography at the moment is framed in terms that decisively juxtapose what are taken, on the one hand, as "global" or at least broadly "non-local" and typically reified and disembodied forces such as "modernization," against what may be described as, at times, resilient and, at others, accommodating strategies taken by persons observed at the "local" level where any impact of such otherwise abstract "forces" are experienced by everyday people. This is to say, in part, that in today's ethnography, comparison tends to productively complicate rather than reductively simplify.

Long-term engagement in the ethnographic fieldwork setting is often termed "participant-observation." We may think of ethnographic research as a continuum wherein there are more or less intense or committed relationships between the ethnographer and those persons who could call "home" what we as field researchers would refer to as "the field." Some projects are intended only as "rapid assessment," entailing only brief, highly focused, decidedly purposeful encounters in the context of what is typically policy-targeted, community-based engagements. Other projects, more typically "academic" in nature, may require months or even years of gradual relationship building and exploration to come to some kind of fulfillment, including applications beyond dissemination of findings alone. For the most part, I am trained in and speaking to particulars that more readily characterize projects consisting of lasting commitments. It is in the practice of participant-observation that more fully adheres to the long-term end of the ethnographic continuum that we find the primary source of rich ethnographic data and the thick description referred to earlier.

Bronislaw Malinowski, the British-trained anthropologist whose work in an early period of professionalization in the discipline during the first half of the twentieth century helped to define the practice, asserted that the ethnographer should not stand apart from those studied. He advocated for engaging participation at a time when some other scholars adhered more strictly to dispassionate observation—even avoiding, in some cases, contact with the field and the actual people under study in favor of using whatever data could be brought to them from sites both near and far. In so doing, these scholars practiced what came to be referred to generally, and pejoratively, as "armchair" anthropology for those most distant from the action and "verandah" anthropology for those who were in-country but happy to remain comfortably ensconced on the well-appointed front porches of current or former colonial powers from whom many anthropologists, of all stripes, very likely received funds for their work.

Writing in the forward to what might be his most well-known ethnography, Malinowski (1922, 3) asserts that "I consider that only such ethnographic sources are of unquestionable scientific value, in which we can clearly draw the line between, on the one hand, the results of direct observation and of native statements and inter-pretations, and on the other, the inferences of the author." The term "participant-observation" is meant to convey what is generally understood to be the dual-role played by an ethnographer. In an explanation of ethnographic fieldwork common to anthropological textbooks, students are told that in order to develop an understand-ing of what it is like to live and work in a given setting—a particular cultural context—the researcher must become a willing, empathetic *participant* in the life of the setting even while maintaining what might be construed as a simultaneous stance of *observer*, or someone who ultimately describes and thus represents the experience with a measure of what we might call "detachment." Such a thoughtfully positioned researcher—operating in the moment of representation within lines clearly drawn—could, it is presumed, provide the sort of ethnographic account that Malinowski would find of undeniable scientific value.

What might not be clearly conveyed to the novice, or even appreciated by Malinowski, however, is that this position is founded on a dynamic, necessarily self-reflexive relationship that must be continually re-balanced by the ethnographer in an ongoing process of engrossing discovery that entails learning not only about people who may be thought to constitute "the Other," and whose degree of "otherness" is purposefully diminished over time, but also learning about "the Self." Barbara Tedlock submits that cultural anthropology since the days of Malinowski has shifted from a largely unexamined reliance on participant observation to a critical "observation of participation." Whereas participant observant ethnographers, as I have suggested, have been tasked to attempt simultaneous engagement and dispassion, in the observation of participation "ethnographers both experience and observe their own and other's *co-participation* within the ethnographic encounter [. . . in what constitutes] a representational transformation in which, instead of a choice between writing an ethnographic memoir centering on the Self or a standard monograph centering on the Other, both Self and Other are presented together within a single narrative ethnography, focused on the character and process of the ethnographic *dialogue*" (Tedlock 1991, 69; emphasis added).

I think that most contemporary cultural anthropologists, at least, would assert that a dualistic role for the researcher—involving at least some measure of the seeming obligatory "distance" that comes with endeavors of a "true" science—does not mean that ethnographers ultimately cannot also speak to the potentially transformative nature of fieldwork or, in being transformed as persons while in the field, become willing advocates for people who are the "subjects" of their study. Speaking of a broad call within anthropology for greater perceived relevancy to the public, Barbara Rylko-Bauer (2006, 186) and her co-authors assert that, in order to achieve this goal, ethnographers and others must have "a willingness to take stands on pressing human issues, to be ethically and politically subjective while methodologically objective, and to accept advocacy (however it is being defined) as part of a disciplinary framework that already values theory and research excellence."

For at least some of the students in my introductory classes, the concept of "cultural relativism" may be interpreted inappropriately as a *moral* relativism. In my attempts to clarify how anthropologists operationalize the concept in the field, I refer to how cultural relativism should serve as a *methodological* relativism that allows for greater empathy and understanding on the part of the researcher. This candidness further assists in creating the basis for an essential "rapport" between people—working together equitably—that comes with mutual trust. In ethnography generally, the "subjective" and "objective" need not be mutually exclusive. In what could be called *critical* ethnography, in particular, they cannot. In the critically-engaged ethnographer's eye, concern for power, privilege and/or biases (what might be called the "positionality") of the ethnographer in relationships with others in the field helps drive a self-reflexive interplay or engagement with participants in research (who may in this particular methodological context be called "collaborators" or "consultants") that is manifest through an open, ongoing dialogue that shapes the meaning and direction of research (e.g., see Lassiter, Hoey, and Campbell 2020). This collaborative approach can extend further still to encompass the manner of dissemination and application of the products of research.

As suggested by Elizabeth Campbell and Luke Eric Lassiter "the explicitly intersubjective practice of contemporary critical ethnography [. . .] brings formerly partitioned processes into inevitable confluence" (2010, 378). Quoting George Marcus (1999, 18 in ibid.), Campbell and Lassiter note that for what might be a majority of ethnographers today, "having to shift personal positions in relation to one's subjects and other active discourses in fields that overlap with one's own, generates a sense of doing more than just traditional ethnography, and it provides a sense of being an activist in even the most 'apolitical' fieldworker." Typically, ethnographers spend many months or even years in the places where they conduct their research, often forming lasting, even lifetime, bonds with people with whom they work in the field. The significance of what I take to be the unavoidable personal involvement of the ethnographer is something to which I return later.

Due to historical development and disciplinary biases, in the past many anthropological ethnographers conducted their research in foreign countries while largely discounting the potential for work at home. I experienced bias first hand as a graduate student in the mid-1990s at the University of Michigan. At least one potential committee member rejected my invitation to serve as advisor on my proposed research in the American Midwest on the grounds that my proposed research—among middle-class, white Americans—was inherently a "less than" form of ethnographic research when compared to what I was made to understand was innately more interesting and important work that could be conducted among an axiomatic Other in distant, self-evidently exotic lands abroad.[3] If all else failed, a would-be cultural anthropologist might consider a domestic project, but only as might be established in some distinct "subculture" of broader American society in which the researcher could not claim membership. This is at least partly why much ethnographically-oriented research in the United States has been done outside of its disciplinary home. Increasing numbers of cultural anthropologists, however, are now doing fieldwork in the communities where they themselves live and work—carrying on where earlier anthropologists have always been, but whose work, with some notable exceptions, has received less attention than those doing research abroad. Or, as I suggested, doing work among subcultural groups at home who are held as somehow mysterious or significantly different from either the putative mainstream of society or, potentially, from the researcher.

Ethnographers collect data that depend on the specific nature of the field setting and, to varying degrees, on the particulars of the project including initial objectives and orienting questions. In addition to such things as observations of behavior, recordings of conversations (including what may be formal, but typically "open-ended" or "unstructured" interviews), and photographs, data may take the form of government reports, newspaper and magazine articles, and representative artifacts that are interpreted to embody characteristics of a topic of interest. Although they may not be tied to the site of study, secondary academic sources may be utilized to "locate" the specific study in terms of theory, methods, population, or geography (among other aspects) within an existing body of literature. An essential source—and one that may go wholly or, at least, largely unacknowledged—is the ethnographer him or herself. I will now turn to the ethnographer as person and discuss more fully the unavoidable centrality of the researcher in the conduct of this particular form of fieldwork.

Exchanging: What is the Ethnographer's Relationship to the Practice of Ethnography?

I like to start my undergraduate course in ethnographic methods by having students define what they believe constitutes a "method."

A stimulating and free-wheeling discussion typically ensues. In the context of this conversation, having identified most of the elements that we would, as scientists, consider to be essential parts of a broad multi-disciplinary definition, we turn somewhat implicitly to thinking about the researcher positioned as "animator" in the conduct of fieldwork research that is often seen as a lifeless methodology. At this point, I have taken some pleasure in informing my students that they are, manifestly, the primary tool of their ethnographic research. At least one student has, understandably, taken issue with the implication that he was, in any way, a "tool." Such things as "interviewing" or even "participant-observation" are often described as individual tools in a reputed methodological "toolkit" figuratively lugged by the ethnographer into the field to enable what might be envisioned as interpersonal procedures of a fundamentally mechanical nature. However, I am committed to the idea that the principal tool—if we are to speak at all of such a thing—must be understood as the ethnographer as a living, breathing, and feeling person engaged in meaningful relationships with other equally real persons. Typically, at about this time in our collective musings, I pull out my dog-eared copy of *Stranger and Friend*, the anthropological memoir of Malinowski's student Hortense Powdermaker and read aloud the following passage from her opening, background chapter.

> The anthropologist is a *human instrument* studying other human beings and their societies. Although he [*sic*] has developed techniques that give him considerable objectivity, it is an illusion for him to think he can remove his personality from his work and become a faceless robot or machinelike recorder of human events. It is important to accept that this human instrument is as much a product of biological, psychological, and social conditioning as are the people he studies (1966, 19; emphasis added).

During the last few decades of the twentieth century, interest has grown noticeably within anthropology for considering the close relationship between personal history, motivation, and the particulars of ethnographic fieldwork. This turn in the discipline was precipitated by several strands of critical self-examination and may as well have shared origins with a simultaneous movement to which Lewis Langness and Gelya Frank refer in the opening to their book *Lives: An Anthropological Approach to Biography*. In this work, Langness and Frank address the rising use of a life-history approach within a decidedly "person-centered" ethnography described as "a rigorous yet compassionate effort on the part of American scholars and others to portray the lives of ordinary individuals [. . .] with the kind of perceptiveness and detail that transform a stranger we might meet in our personal lives into a friend" (1981, 1).

While Langness and Frank are referring to the subject(s) of ethnographic inquiry, which is to say the people with whom we work in the field, they also speak to a larger turn in the discipline toward "reflexivity"—the principle that the same theories of knowledge used to understand others can be self-consciously applied to understanding the construction of those theories themselves, if not also ourselves as willful participants in this construction. A person-centered research focus is thought to reveal, through intimate personal details, broadly relevant features of the culture and society that shape the conditions that give rise to characteristic life histories. The approach is naturally *biographical* in nature. At the same time, Langness and Frank explain that "Getting to know any person in depth is a major experience [for both parties] because we have to admit that another way of structuring the world truly exists" (ibid.). Thus, in what must be acknowledged as a shared experience, we are presented with the fundamentally *autobiographical* as when the ethnographer him or herself turns to examining the significance of their own involvement in the lives of others and their positionality, at least partly, relative to the persons with whom they are working. Here we understand that this encounter among persons, and any account that emerges as a distinct life history, for example, is a complex, self-constituting *negotiation* between people with their own variously shared and distinct needs and desires.

A volume suggestively titled *Anthropology and Autobiography*, edited by Judith Okely and Helen Callaway (1992), helped to frame an emerging debate about reflexivity and the professional ethical obligations of the ethnographer who, despite being long proclaimed *participant*-observer, had historically made only limited, formalized appearances in the products of those works. That is to say, the ethnographer may have been presented as one of the actors on the stage, but we were given little insight into his or her background (what might be going on "backstage") or sense of an inner life in the manner that we have come to expect of "others" portrayed in an ethnographic account.

I first took seriously the relationship between life story, fieldwork, and scholarship when constructing an intellectual biography of anthropologist Roy Rappaport for a posthumous *American Ethnologist* article based on his fond, end-of-life recollections as well as tender regrets of fieldwork in Papua New Guinea as he succumbed to lung cancer in 1997 (Hoey and Fricke 2007). I came to understand that it is undeniably important to question and understand how these elements have bearing on the construction of theory and, ultimately, the conduct of an academic life. What I learned from my experience working with Rappaport and my co-author, Tom Fricke, was that unforeseen encounters along circuitous paths, personal and professional experiences, together with historical context, lead individual researchers to their particular topical foci and a set of methodological and theoretical approaches.

Roger Sanjek (2014; see also Sanjek 2015) also argues that the anthropologist as ethnographer and social theorist exerts an autobiographical agency by virtue of how one's past motivates and thus shapes present choices. These choices include what issues to study; how to interpret significance in conversations, observed events, and experiences while in the field (at least some of which come from the unique sociocultural "terrain" of the field site itself); and ultimately how to engage with one's scholarly audience and a greater public. Sanjek holds that "ethnography is inescapably lodged in the social worlds of those who use it" (ibid., ix), but that this is appropriate given that ethnographers today work to reveal and, to whatever extent possible, control or at least account for and not deny, their possible biases. In his own case, Sanjek asserts a "cohort effect" associated with coming of age as an anthropologist in 1960s New York City at Columbia University surrounded by some of the most influential contributors to our field, including most conspicuously Marvin Harris—an effect shared, I will note, with Rappaport.

Theory too, Sanjek avows, is autobiographical as it is critical in shaping and molding the ethnographic process, just as fieldwork enables us as researchers to develop theory. In some ways, the most compelling aspect of *Ethnography in Today's World* is Sanjek's autobiographical tales of a prominent anthropologist born out of the urban, counter-cultural tumult of the civil rights era who matured to navigate and respond to the theoretical storms and impact of 1980s postmodernism—at least some of which he found agreeable, for example, in the call for more critically self-conscious approaches. However, he decries much of this turn toward reflexivity as leading to lost relevance for the discipline outside of (and even within) academia as a result of postmodernism's most ardent proponents deciding to abandon traditions of broad contextualization (i.e., tracing layers of history and political economy in the setting of complex global flows) and comparative analysis (i.e., where an outstanding problem of theory is systematically addressed using ethnographic data from different places and times).[4]

In order to appreciate the extent to which the ethnographer is personally involved in long-term fieldwork engagement, I will at least begin to explore an intersection between the lives of those participating in the production of knowledge in and through ethnographic fieldwork—that is to say, both the ethnographer and those with whom he or she necessarily collaborates as voluntary participants in that work. Therefore, I must consider ways in which the researcher may be personally challenged and changed by the experience of fieldwork as well as how fieldwork can be informative to personal narratives—the life stories—of those engaged in it as participants.

As I have clarified here, my position has long been that ethnographic fieldwork is shaped by personal and professional identities just as these identities are inevitably shaped by individual experiences while in the field. Unfortunately, the autobiographical dimension of ethnographic research has been downplayed historically if not discounted altogether. More recently, so-called autoethnography has emerged as a response, perhaps, to this possible failing within the literature as well as to introduce new—though not uncontroversial—dimensions to the range of practice of ethnographic fieldwork (e.g., Reed-Danahay 1997). I take contributions of this approach to be at least partly representative of recognition by these scholars of the inevitability of the Self in fieldwork generally as well as a specific contribution to the literature on ethnographic methods regarding another potential "instrument" in the putative, shared methodological "toolkit." Unlike "self-narrative" writings such as memoir, autoethnography explicitly applies a cultural analysis and interpretation of the researcher's own behaviors, thoughts, and experiences while engaged with others in a given sociocultural context.[5] That is to say, proponents of this method employ much the same means—at least analytically speaking—and have the intent to arrive at the same ends as more traditional ethnographic research.

For the most part, and despite the development of autoethnographic studies, the autobiographical continues to be restrained in accounts of ethnographic fieldwork. This is perhaps the consequence a perceived threat to the objectivity that most people expect of a legitimate science and to the supposed reliability of our data if we appear as researchers to permit subjectivity to intervene by allowing the ethnographer's encumbered persona to appear instead of adhering to the presumed role of a largely (if not wholly) dispassionate observer. But can it ever be said of any research—whether in the field or in the lab—that emotion is not constitutive of practice? That is to say, emotions are not simply a consequence of the practice of research—or, in the context of my discussion, at least, something that merely *happens* to us as researchers in the field (cf. Davies and Spencer 2010). As described by Robert Solomon (1978, 187), emotion is "a network of conceptual and perceptual structures in which the objects and people in our world, others' actions and our own, are given significance."

This simple truth was—in the context of ethnographic fieldwork—brought to revealing and heart-wrenching light in the account of Renato Rosaldo's (1993) research among Ilongot people in the Philippines where he lost his wife, Michelle, to a horrific and sudden death by falling from a cliff while they were together in the field. Rosaldo conveys that it was only through his profound loss, the experience of what he describes as an "emotional force of bereavement," and the subsequent change in his subject position relative to the Ilongot behaviors that he observed in the field (including the practice of grieving Ilongot men taking human heads), that he was able to grasp the significance of his own observations, the motivations of the Ilongot, and the need for cultural descriptions to seek out and convey qualities of emotional force as well as the representational "thickness" to which Geertz refers. For Rosaldo (1993, 2), a "gradual thickening of symbolic webs of meaning" alone and without emotion, may not lead to sufficient elaboration and subsequent understanding.

With the simplicity of Solomon's understanding regarding the formative nature of emotion in our understanding of the world and the force of Rosaldo's illustration, we may reflect generally on how we interpret events and find meaning as researchers at least partly through emotion, whether boredom or surprise, fear or delight. That is, emotion is not merely a reaction to what happens to us. This is true of people generally, whether researchers or not. In the context of research, the very questions that we seek to answer through our work express both professional and personal desires, if even it makes sense to distinguish these as independent domains. In the case of ethnographic fieldwork, we seek so that we may find—or not find— answers to our open questions through our experience as human beings participating in relationships with other human beings. Our seeking unavoidably entails emotion and, thus, personal involvement such that, more so than with many other methodologies, the personal and the professional are only artificially and retroactively separated.

Most anthropologists today point to Malinowski as a kind of "founding father" to ethnographic fieldwork and the practice of participant-observation. Malinowski's early twentieth-century ethnographies were written in a voice removed and largely unrevealing about the ethnographer in the context of his real or imagined relationships to people that he studied. Since Malinowski's time, the personal account of fieldwork has been customarily hidden away in unpublished marginal notes and diaries. These "off the record" writings, however, document tacit impressions and emotional experiences without which we cannot, as ethnographers, fully appreciate and understand the project of our research itself. For many ethnographers, then as today, "fieldnotes" (to which I return later) are composed of what might be thought of as that writing that is thought to constitute "data." All other writing, including a "diary" of experiences, would be considered separately as the "non-data" elements of being human as a researcher in the context of doing scientific fieldwork.

My position has always been that the accounts we provide of our fieldwork in the form of our findings are based on information we have been able to gather only through investing ourselves in real, human relationships. These fieldwork relationships may not be entirely "normal" by the measures of any person's everyday life, given the particular circumstances for their formation and continuance within the purposeful nature of a research project—just as an interview isn't a typical conversation—but they are relationships just the same. Therefore, the emotionally informed nature of these relationships is arguably as significant to the ethnographic writing we produce as are the data we collect. Without one, we would not have the other. Despite what Malinowski contributed to the practice of cultural anthropology in terms of defining an intersecting, simultaneous role of participant-observer, his countervailing legacy to the ethnographic method is an artificial and retroactive separation between the "fieldwork" experience and the (often geographically, as well as emotionally, distant) experience of "writing up," the results of that work in the professionally acceptable format required for scholarly dissemination.

Although, as I have stressed, what we know as ethnographers is inseparable from our relationships in and out of the context of fieldwork, much ethnographic writing does some harm to those relationships by imposing or, at least, re-imposing boundaries between self and other. This creates a tension to which we might, increasingly, expect a response by our coparticipants. Because of the very real familiarity of these relationships and the expectations that come part and parcel in the context of such significant contact between people, those with whom we work in the field can and do, more and more, confront representations of our relationships and their lives and may find some fault. This confrontation may be born of a serious sense of broken confidence or, perhaps, a violation of complex realities of particular lived experience and relationships that we—as ethnographers and as human beings—claim to, at least partly, share.

As for Malinowski, his emotive diaries—replete with feelings of deep loneliness, self-doubt, sexual frustration, and fear—were published only after his death in a revealing autobiographical account of his inner life while in the field (*A Diary in the Strict Sense of the Term*, first published in 1967). No doubt these diaries were essential to Malinowski, even if he restricted them to tacitly shaping the form of writings and conclusions that would appear in publicly disseminated work. Among other things, we learn in these diaries that Malinowski longed to write great novels even as his scientific writing effectively defined the fieldwork approaches of cultural anthropology for much of the twentieth century. Malinowski was a storyteller in fact and at heart.

Of their possible lessons, Malinowski's diaries hold two of special relevance here. The first of these is that, fundamentally, ethnographic writing is a means of expressing a shared interest among human beings for telling stories—stories about what it means to be human. The second is that the explicit professional project of observing, imagining, and describing other people needs not be incompatible with the implicit personal project of learning about the Self. It is the dependable truth of fieldwork that these two projects—these two narratives—are always implicated in each other. Ethnographic fieldwork involves more than just the outward trials and tribulations of building rapport with "the locals" and getting to know "the local" whoever and wherever we find ourselves. In my ideal, at least, it should entail an inward journey of self-discovery. Good ethnography recognizes the potentially transformative nature of fieldwork where as we search for answers to questions about other people we come to find ourselves in their stories.

What I am speaking to here is akin to what Carolyn Ellis, much as Tedlock, refers to as "interactive introspection" wherein "the researcher works back and forth with others to assist in their introspection, but the object of study is the emergent experiences of both parties. Interactive introspection provides self-introspection from subject and researcher, since a researcher must introspect about her own responses in reaction to experiences and feelings" of those with whom he or she works (Ellis 1991, 30). Regardless of the extent to which anyone is changed by the experience of their encounter, ethnography should be acknowledged as a mutual, exchanged product born of connected, intertwining lives of the ethnographer and those people on whom he or she come to rely while in the field. In this, as in much of what I am attempting to convey about contemporary ethnographic fieldwork, the person with whom we have a relationship in the field—who has generally been referred to as "Other," to convey cultural distance, "subject," to passively position relative to the act of research, or "informant," to suggest a more active but still distant role—should rightly, in an inclusive and authentic way, be thought of as, at least, a "co-participant" in the process and very likely what Lassiter suggests should be a "co-researcher" (2005).

Despite pleadings of my undergraduate students for some kind of "formula" to save them from the apparent, near existential, angst associated with undertaking their own first ethnographic fieldwork projects, I have persisted in my conviction that ethnography is often less a method than it is what we might have to call an *anti-method*— at least insofar as we typically define a method as an organized plan that predetermines how something is done. That is to say, fieldwork practice does not entail performing from a virtual script. Rather, it is more accurately and, arguably at its best, improvisational and dependent, in no small amount, on *serendipity*. In doing this work, then, we must be open and even "vulnerable." Ruth Behar (1996) called for such vulnerability in her eloquently-stated call for a progressively more humanistic and impactful anthropology as compensation for what may have long been an excessive degree of abstraction and depersonalization in published ethnographic accounts.

Behar describes the practice of ethnography as an "irreversible voyage" where the ethnographer necessarily goes "elsewhere," but never simply by making a physical trip to another place, and whose journey is captured in a reflexive portrayal in which the ethnographer "inscribes the self" into the account through the autobiographical. By being what we take as more "subjective" and, ultimately, "vulnerable," Behar suggests a path toward a more truthful—or perhaps "authentic" in the manner most valued by presumptive objectivity in science—perspective from which to understand what we have come to learn from those with whom we work and, ultimately, from which to represent our own fieldwork experience. Importantly, there must be some kind of limits placed here in order for the product of such work to remain within the domain of social science. Speaking to such limits, Behar (1996, 14) rightly notes that "Vulnerability doesn't mean that anything personal goes" but rather that "exposure of the self who is also a spectator [i.e., the observer] has to take us somewhere we couldn't otherwise get to. It has to be essential to the argument, not a decorative flourish, not exposure for its own sake [. . . such that] a personal voice, if creatively used, can lead the reader, not into miniature bubbles of navel-gazing, but into the enormous sea of serious social issues."

Ethnographic fieldwork is always a unique and emerging combination of the researcher and the particular circumstances and personal relationships born of and in the field. So, I would counsel my students, you must embrace the serendipitous encounter that rouses subjective feelings more than you may feel the need to cling to what might seem reassuring, prescribed steps of a would-be dispassionate science. I contend that the emotional attachments we may make while in the field, together with our willingness to be honest with ourselves about the nature of our experience and their impact on our work, actually produce an understanding not only of others but also ourselves that is more sympathetic, humane, and ultimately accurate in terms of representing what it means to be human.

Impacting: What Kinds of Influence Does Such a Method Have?

Despite a broad public misconception about the discipline—perhaps born of partial understandings of the principle of cultural relativism —that ethnographers should have no lasting influence (either negative or positive) on those persons who are the subject of their studies, cultural anthropologists have long sought to have impact in the lives of others through varying degrees of collaboration in the conduct of fieldwork with the intent, for example, of creating action plans that may affect public policy and change the course of community development. But what of the unintended impact of our encounters on the lives of those with whom ethnographers work? These effects are typically unacknowledged given, perhaps, how they lie outside explicit research agendas. Do we take these effects to be simply things that may happen naturally in the dialogic exchange among mutually interested persons who may, over time, develop a relationship that goes beyond brief meetings contrived by the researcher to collect data in the context of research?

During my long-term project in Northern Michigan, I became (though only informally) interested in how the personal narratives of project participants might be shaped through our relationship over time. My particular project may be largely responsible for this interest. As an examination of how people can deliberately use the act of relocation—often coupled with significant changes in work and family life—as a way of remaking self-identity, my study meant that I was working with people who were actively engaged in personal identity formation as a deliberative process. It seemed to me that as I worked with them, I became a part of their ongoing inner and outer conversations in this effort. While I clearly needed them for the purposes of my research, it seemed to me that they had a self-conscious need to engage in retrospective as well as prospective dialogue about their decision making. It seemed that I was serving a purpose in their lives—my role in the fieldwork relationship was valuable and valued.

I was purposefully seeking knowledge in a general, scientific way. I wanted to know why people were doing what they were doing. I was going about discovering what appeared to be the factors that shaped particular beliefs and behaviors over time. At the same time, the people with whom I worked were seeking personal insight and engaged in sense-making in a very purposeful way. Among other things, they wanted to know if what they were doing made sense to others and they wanted to learn what meaning their decisions might have in the broader social and cultural context that they believed I might—given my posture as a social scientist—understand somehow more fully or even, perhaps, dispassionately than them. That is, they appeared to seek what we might call, in everyday terms, "perspective." At least initially, participants sought me out as some kind of impartial expert. More often than not, they told me that it was helpful to them to have someone outside family and friends who would listen, without judgment, to their stories of personal struggle. In not only listening but also in sharing my own personal struggles while in the field, I helped them to learn about others who made similar decisions. This knowledge clearly helped to shape their continuously emerging sense of self (e.g., see Hoey 2005). As our encounters grew in number, they learned about my work with others and would tell me things like, "It's good to know that we're not alone." We can easily find ourselves in this basic human desire for what could be called "belonging," which was, itself, a basic motivation for many behaviors observed in my study population.

Without my suggestion, some came to see themselves while we talked over the course of many conversations as part of some kind of larger "movement" of people who were somehow challenging status quo assumptions about what it meant to live the "good life" in America at the start of the twenty-first century. I did not attempt to disavow them of this thought. For one thing, I wasn't all that sure of my position; I was still learning. When I have followed up periodically over the years with these people who are now at least very good acquaintances if not true friends, they tell me that it is good to be reminded of their original plans and intentions as they set out to make lifestyle changes through relocation and remake work and family arrangements in the process. It seems that they have come to rely on me—in some small way, at least—to help find and maintain their bearings over time. I may provide a common thread as they go about the work of mapping out a trajectory for their present life, in part, out of what we have shared in the past. I know they found the times that we spent together meaningful and affirming to the narratives they have come to tell themselves about the purpose and direction of their lives. Indeed, accounts within the broad literature on qualitative research methods suggests that participants often find ethnographic interviewing provides opportunities for healthful introspection and what some might characterize as personal growth (e.g., Frank 2000; Ortiz 2001).[6]

The oral historian Valerie Yow (2005) speaks to meaning making in how people who are engaged in our research interpret their experience and how researchers interject themselves in this process as both participant-observers and narrators. More broadly, any researchers—and perhaps especially ethnographers—by their very presence in the field help to shape the phenomena they observe. I have always contended that such "reactive effects" or "consequential practice"—as termed by Robert Emerson and his coauthors (2011) in their excellent book on the writing of fieldnotes—that is, how people respond to our presence, are themselves important forms of data that should not be seen as somehow "contaminating" what we may observe, experience, and learn in the field. Rather, these effects, as long as we become conscious of them, could well provide a source for our learning.

John Van Maanen reminds us that ethnographies are themselves narratives and—as with the narratives of individuals included within those texts—are experientially driven and purposefully shaped. The interpretive process entailed in going from fieldwork data to written account (i.e., what is ultimately disseminated to others in various ways) is about rendering the experiences of those participating in the research as well as those conducting that research into representative texts—a process that begins with capturing them in the context of our fieldnotes. As a broader context for this point, Van Maanen (1988, ix) has gone so far as to assert that ethnography "is the peculiar practice of representing the social reality of others through the analysis of one's own experience in the world of these others." This is very close to an observation by Clifford Geertz (1988, 10) that ethnography depends on "the oddity of constructing texts ostensibly scientific out of experiences broadly biographical." Despite this odd or, perhaps, necessary tension, Geertz felt that ethnography rightly held a claim to truth about the nature of human life that research founded on exaggeratedly construed objectivity, characteristic of approaches akin to positivism, could not.

Although concerned specifically with documentary fieldwork,

Robert Coles has shown how any attempt at representation of lived experience is necessarily an interpretation despite the fact that there is a tendency among readers or viewers of such work to accept it at face value—to view it as a somehow autonomous reality. A child psychiatrist and author of numerous books concerned with human moral and spiritual reasoning, Cole suggests plainly that "objectivity" is a myth. Representation of life necessarily entails some subjective distortion given that the lived world is complex and ambiguous when compared with the relative simplicity and neatness required of an account of the research on which it is based. In the end, Coles (1997, 250) asserts that it is "Through selection, emphasis and the magic of narrative art, [that] the reader or viewer gets convincingly close to a scene, a subject matter and sees the documentary as one of many possible takes, not the story, but a story."

Before turning, finally, to some practicalities of ethnographic fieldnotes upon which any account of the field is based, I would like to finalize my examination in this section by summarizing my point that, within this peculiar practice of ethnographic fieldwork, an entwining of narrative selves is arguably both necessary and desirable if we are to tell a story that convincingly reflects the reality of human social life. I understand that my position and the arguments for and against it are not entirely novel. Yet, it is helpful for me— if not those still in training—to be reminded that unique insight, however small, into what it means to be human may be found at the intersection of the biographical and the autobiographical in ethnographic fieldwork.

What is the Role of Fieldnotes in the Practice of Ethnography?

I have written this chapter both for my students (and they will likely hear what I have to say here in some form even if I don't hand them a copy of this chapter to read) and for those who may be newly discovering or, perhaps, rediscovering the practice of ethnography. It is not meant to be a "how to" guide in any measure. Yet, I have intended to speak to how one might productively orient oneself to the practice and think about (as I tell my students) what it might "feel like" to do ethnography. My ideal is that this feeling should emerge in ethnographic practice that is fully engaged in what is likely (for my undergraduates) "the local" and in the particular manner that I have suggested in this chapter will capture at least some of its revealing (in the sense of discovering or recovering knowledge) and transformative (in the sense of having meaningful and practical impact that begins at the level of personal relationships born of the fieldwork encounter) potentials. Given that so much of ethnographic fieldwork depends on the researcher's own experience and perspective, the "I" must be acknowledged. It really does matter where you as a researcher "stand" relative to the process of your own fieldwork and ultimately to the "subject" of your study. Such an understanding involves not only whether you might consider yourself an "insider" or an "outsider" to a group that may be your focus, but also the attitudes and/or preconceptions you bring to that study. This is true of any science regardless of whether a tension between "objectivity" and "subjectivity" is acknowledged or conveniently ignored as a non-issue after the proper rituals of research are performed. In any event, it is unavoidably true that there must be an acknowledged "I" in ethnographic fieldwork.

If you are judgmental in your treatment of what or whom you are studying, this will affect the product of your work by influencing the process—your capacity to accurately capture details thickly described in the fieldnotes that become your data, to interpret that data, and to represent (in some measure) the lives of others as well as the account of your fieldwork as something that you, yourself, experienced. That much seems clear. However, it is more than this. I have found that many students in ethnographic training are reluctant at best and, at times, highly critical of the demands that ethnographic work places on them. Frankly, these students may resent the time and energy that doing this kind of fieldwork requires—especially within fragmented, overloaded schedules. Doing this work can disrupt one's everyday life—not to mention a carefully manufactured plan for a semester. I must tell them that if they are judgmental of the process by being dismissive of the work that they are doing, this can be harmful and insidiously distortive. One needs to be open-minded and thus allow for possibilities for insight and discovery to emerge. If my students say "nothing happened" in their fieldnote journal for a given visit to a fieldwork site, they have likely shut off any possibility that there was, in fact, something there of significance to at least witness and even experience. We may attribute this rush to dismissive labeling of both observed phenomena and one's own experience, at least in part, to not seeing what one has come to take for granted. This problem is likely compounded by familiarity with a local site and, in some measure, a contributing factor to the disciplinary bias for foreign sites to which I spoke earlier. That is to say, taking things for granted is an especially problematic tendency for those of us who work within our own culture(s) and communities.

Ethnographic fieldwork is challenging in a multitude of ways that are, frankly, not well understood to those who either know nothing of its practice or may know only enough to believe, wrongly, that it consists only of "hanging out, talking to people, and taking notes." Ethnographic fieldwork is also immensely rewarding when we allow for its transformative potential. In the context of my undergraduate course in ethnographic methods, I ask students to keep certain things in mind. For example, while we can and should acknowledge our methodological and other challenges—e.g., these could become at least some of the "limitations" of a study that are productively addressed within any report on that research—it is not a good idea to write in a consistently negative way about the work in which we are engaged. The real, emotionally-charged frustration experienced by students can lead to snap judgments and to thinking that tends to lump people and their beliefs and behaviors into stereotyped categories. It is entirely possible to have a less-than-stellar ethnographic fieldwork or fieldwork-training experience. This might be objectively measured by how well a student is able to practically collect sufficient data with which to work through cultural interpretation and analysis and whether they are able to draw credible, plausible, and possibly transferable conclusions from that work— that is, to produce an ethnography. At the subjective level, success may be measured by the student's feelings about their fieldwork experience and, for example, whether it has lived up to their own expectations. When students arrive at the end of their time in the field (or at least in our semester-long ethnographic methods course together) and are weighed down by what are subjectively negative experiences, I reassure them that these experiences may still be analyzed for their potential contribution to a discussion about the emotional and practical challenges of ethnographic fieldwork generally. Simply stated, we can learn from challenging experience if it is examined for personal and professional insight.

One of the greatest challenges for students of ethnography is coming to understand that doing an ethnography is not at all like doing research based on books or articles—what is typically referred to as "secondary" research. Although as a student (and even a credentialed scholar) it is possible to neglect secondary research writing until the proverbial last minute, such a strategy is a simple recipe for disaster when doing ethnographic fieldwork. One cannot wait until the end of the process to "write up" an ethnography—a comprehensive report or account of that work. Ethnographic fieldwork is *primary* research and is thus very different to what college students (and others) may be used to in doing *secondary* research.

Ethnographers in training are told to keep something with them at all times in which they can jot down observations and impressions. This can be a small (pocket-sized) notebook or even a folded piece of paper. I have made notes on any number of different scraps of paper on hand at the time that I realize that I need to begin the process of making sense of something that I have encountered. I continuously remind my students that they must work from such in-the-field jottings to create more detailed fieldnotes that "flesh out" what might be little more than bullet points. Some people nowadays use a small voice recorder to record impressions. I would still think it necessary to get that information out of the recorder (and also out of our heads) and into some textual form in order to make representations of experience in the field and effectively work with the data.

One of the most essential purposes for writing fieldnotes is, as Geertz would say, to turn the events of the moment into an *account* that can be consulted again (and again) later. Among other things, that account allows for the ethnographer to commit what he or she might not know is important in that moment to memory. We often will not know what is important until later, after other information and insight has been provided by further experience and exploration in the field. If one does not adequately document things now, they will likely not be available later apart from even more partial recollections than what is available to us in and through our necessarily limited fieldnotes. Immediately following from documentation is the opportunity to recognize *patterns*. Are there things that people say or do, for example, that suggest consistencies or relationships that are somehow ordered? Does something seem to be a "ritual," for example? I tell my students that rituals are not far-out or exotic things. They happen all around us—not only in churches but also football stadiums. They are apparent in town meetings and college classrooms. You can find them in the bathroom as well as the bedroom. They're everywhere. Here, I often suggest that my students take a look at Horace Miner's (1956) article "Body Ritual among the Nacirema" for mischievous insight into how we can make the familiar unfamiliar and therefore both noticeable and more readily subject to our analysis and interpretation.

As I have suggested, ethnographers can spend a good long time (months at least) working in the field so that they can, in much of this work, discover their purpose through lengthy participant-observation. This is why we so often hear ethnographic research referred to as "emergent" or as taking place "from the ground up." In most undergraduate courses in ethnographic methods, students should be given a set of training experiences that at least approach what would be typical of the professional ethnographer. In most cases, however, instructors cannot duplicate the full rigors of fieldwork for practical reasons—there is simply not enough time. Courses should be structured to allow for lots of exploration of the experience of participant-observation and the interactive and iterative process of revisiting what is collected in fieldnotes in order to continually refine one's understanding and approach. When a subject is raised—often as a question about a particular group or a cultural practice or belief—this begins to give focus and direction to the inquiry and writing. Both become increasingly purposeful. This is why it is so important that students undergo fieldnote reviews throughout the process of instruction.

Ethnographers depend on writing. In keeping with the open-mindedness that comes with the approach in the preliminary stages, ethnographers write about things that interest them generally about their fieldsite. They may even just begin writing about their own lives as a way to raise questions about the world around them. Of course, this facilitates recognition of the relationship between biography and fieldwork—the entwining of narratives that I previously discussed. My first assignment in my undergraduate course in ethnographic methods is, in fact, for students to read the first two chapters from a book on writing memoir by Bill Roorbach. I take pride in the fact that I met Bill and came to know his work while I was a participant at the Bear River Writer's Conference in Northern Michigan in the late 1990s. I was in attendance as an ethnographer in recognition of the fact that in order to do my work well, I needed to know how to write well. In particular, I wanted to write compelling stories. For me that meant not only "learning how to write" in particular ways but also developing a personally-engaged, creative relationship with the act of writing. In the chapters that I share with my students, Roorbach (1998) speaks to such things as the simultaneous centrality and fault-iness of memory as source for identity and the necessity for having an acknowledged, ever-present "I" who constructs what must be—as I want them to recognize ethnography itself—a work of non-fiction that is necessarily "creative."

My students then undertake, following Roorbach's direction, a simple mapping assignment whereby they recall and explore their earliest memories of a place where they grew up and, using this graphical representation of their memory, craft a brief "map story" in which they seek their narrative "voice" and, hopefully, arrive at some recognition of the importance of their own history in coming to account for what it means to be human. At the very least, they have a glimpse into their own culturally- and socially-situated life history, particular and possibly unique as it may be, as an expression of a fun-damental fact of our shared humanity—growing up. In this exercise, I intend to have students come to realize—through their writing of what usually appears to be the utterly mundane (what Malinowski might have called the "imponderabilia of everyday life") and, later, in the sharing of their stories—that significant realizations can be made about themselves in particular sociocultural and historical contexts as well as about the "human condition" generally—including, simply, our propensity for storytelling. To avoid simply ending up with detailed descriptions of maps or the real places that they are presumed to represent—that is to say "camera's eye" depictions that lack interpretation of the possible significance of details—I remind students that the assignment asks for a "story" and thus, by my reckoning at least, something must *happen*.

I follow this "warm up" exercise in writing and thinking about our relationships to memory as well as writing as a representational act with a more overtly fieldwork-related but similar assignment on mapping a (city) block drawn from Paul Kutsche's (1998) book on ethnographic fieldwork methods. My intent is to help students learn how fieldwork must be situated in a particular time and place, inspire them to overcome preconceived notions and perceptions about a given place and avoid judgmental shorthand in their descriptions, and, as always, to learn how to see what is familiar as if it were unfamiliar. As I suggested earlier, how we choose to see (or not see) the world is as important as how we choose to describe it. To help my students to think critically about their ability to observe ordinary things and everyday places in new ways—and to consequently open themselves up to genuine discovery through an enhanced visual and, ultimately, mental agility that facilitates productive, serendipitous encounter—I have them read the opening chapter—appropriately titled "Beginnings"—of John Stilgoe's (1999) *Outside Lies Magic*.

Because fieldnotes chronicle our fieldwork encounters, they are where patterns are allowed to develop. Accordingly, ethnographers rely extensively on them to provide insight into what qualities may define members in a given group, for example. That is, ethnographers depend on their fieldnotes to discover, to work toward preliminary understandings, to develop interpretations, and eventually to reach their conclusions. Ethnography, in large part, may be said to take place in and through fieldnotes. If it isn't in your notes—I like to say—you do not have it. From the beginning of their time in the field, ethnographers are constantly writing up observations and results, drawing at least tentative conclusions that they will continue to revisit in order to continually refine them.

As Geertz has said, ethnographic inquiry is the product of the field of cultural anthropology that is ultimately not an empirical science in search of immutable law, but rather an interpretative one in search of perennially emergent, intersubjective meaning. He further counseled that our understanding as ethnographers was always tentative and that as such we must aim, realistically, for what is productively a further refinement of debate rather than "the final word" on each of those myriads of subjects—collectively thought to contribute to an understanding of the human condition—to which we devote our attention as ethnographers. In this spirit, Renato Rosaldo (1993, 8) has said:

> Although the doctrine of preparation, knowledge, and sensibility contains much to admire, one should work to undermine the false comfort that it can convey. At what point can people say that they have completed their learning or their life experience? The problem with taking this mode of preparing the ethnographer too much to heart is that it can lend a false air of security, an authoritative claim to certitude and finality that our analyses cannot have. All interpretations are provisional; they are made by positioned subjects who are prepared to know certain things [at any given point in time, including when they encounter someone or something in the field, as Rosaldo with the Ilongot,] and not others.

By remaining, as suggested by Rosaldo, "open" in multiple ways as the "human instruments" that we are, in a manner akin to Behar's notion of vulnerability, ethnographers are best positioned for the revelatory and transformational impressions possible in the practice of our methodology and, ultimately, for building relationships through which we can connect meaningfully with others, exchange something important of ourselves, and have practical impact for a common good.

NOTES

1. In fact, Geertz should be credited with popularizing a notion originally described by philosopher Gilbert Ryle (1971) as an account of behavior that permits an understanding (in the reader) that goes beyond surface appearances to describe underlying patterns as well as broader cultural contexts that give that behavior its particular, culturally-informed meaning.

2. As I will explore in some greater detail later, the act of "writing culture" is no simple thing and certainly not one that should be taken for granted. Marking an especially important milestone in an emerging debate within the discipline of anthropology during the 1980s, the book *Writing Culture* (Clifford and Marcus 1986) tackled varied forms of ethnographic writing in terms of reflexivity and objectivity as well as what had been taken heretofore as the essential underpinnings of "ethnographic authority," or what might be conveyed in the seemingly simple assertion of a ethnographer that "I was there," in what had been and was becoming an increasingly and complexly interconnected world wherein, among other things, postcolonialism encouraged the examination of differentials of power between peoples in and from different places. This book helped mark what some refer to as a "turn" in anthropology described variously as "reflexive," "literary," "post-modern," "deconstructive," and "post-structural." The years that I spent in graduate school during the 1990s were a time now considered the height of an ensuing "crisis of representation" provoked by such critical works as *Writing Culture*. Needless to say, the predicament made for stirring exchanges between older and younger faculty in the department who, at times, appeared to be speaking entirely different languages. For my part, contributions to the debate such as *Writing Culture* became helpful only insofar as they helped, over time, to bring attention to what might have been largely unexamined positions in anthropology—which is to say that the actions elicited by these positions might have become "mere" ritual enactments of enduring tradition with regard to basic questions of "who," "what," "where," and "how." By this I mean questions of who is doing the fieldwork (e.g., is the fieldworker "native" to the fieldwork context or not); what topics should be

studied; where should fieldwork be conducted (i.e., what constitutes an appropriate site); how should fieldwork be conducted (e.g., should it be thought of as a collaborative endeavor among equals); and, of course, how the results of fieldwork should be represented.

3. In fact, I ended up doing two dissertation fieldwork projects. The first was far more "traditional" in that I traveled halfway around the globe with a Fulbright fellowship to conduct fieldwork in a remote corner of Indonesia, relying on funds with origins in Cold War-era geopolitical concerns. The second, to which I refer here, was conducted in the state of Michigan through a grant from the Alfred P. Sloan Foundation, relying on funds with origins in the fortunes of the twentieth-century American automobile industry and General Motors. I defended the later project for my doctorate and produced a published ethnography on this work (Hoey 2014).

4. Contextualization and comparison are two sides of what Sanjek refers to as the "anthropological triangle" that serves as an operational system of knowledge construction of which ethnographic fieldwork is the final side and without which—all three aspects interacting—descriptive works of people and place cannot be said to be truly ethnographic. Sanjek traces ways in which, in the past century and a half, anthropologists have variously stressed or neglected different sides of the triangle. He notes, for example, how Franz Boas (in the United States) and Malinowski (in Europe) each declined to provide a larger context to their studies in order to create a fictive "ethnographic present" (i.e., a literary and temporal strategy employed to create a representation of a people prior to "contact" with Europeans) rather than an "ethnography of the present."

5. See Gergen and Gergen (1983) for more on this concept.

6. At the same time, it should be noted, the purposely open-ended nature of many of these conversations allows for the possibility of what could in some instances amount to "unhealthy" introspection leading to a risk of psychological harm through what may be great "emotional distress" (see Corbin and Morse 2016). This possibility concerns not only IRBs but any properly trained researcher, as well. Fortunately, I cannot provide any personal commentary on the impact of such distress, as I have not—at least knowingly—witnessed it in my own fieldwork.

WORKS CITED

Behar, Ruth. 1996. *The Vulnerable Observer: Anthropology that Breaks your Heart*. Boston: Beacon Press.

Campbell, Elizabeth, and Luke Eric Lassiter. 2010. "From Collaborative Ethnography to Collaborative Pedagogy: Reflections on the Other Side of Middletown Project and Community-University Research Partnerships." *Anthropology & Education Quarterly* 41 (4): 370–85.

Clifford, James, and George Marcus. 1986. *Writing Culture: The Poetics and Politics of Ethnography*. Berkeley, CA: University of California Press.

Coles, Robert. 1997. *Doing Documentary Work*. New York: Oxford University Press.

Corbin, Juliet, and Janice M. Morse. 2016. "The Unstructured Interactive Interview: Issues of Reciprocity and Risks when Dealing with Sensitive Topics." *Qualitative Inquiry* 9 (3): 335–54.

Davies, James, and Dimitrina Spencer, eds. 2010. *Emotions in the Field: The Psychology and Anthropology of Fieldwork Experience*. Stanford, CA: Stanford University Press.

Ellis, Carolyn. 1991. "Sociological Introspection and Emotional Experience." *Symbolic Interaction* 14 (1): 23–50.

Emerson, Robert M., Rachel I. Fretz, and Linda L. Shaw. 2011. *Writing Ethnographic Fieldnotes*. Second edition. Chicago Guides to Writing, Editing, and Publishing. Chicago: The University of Chicago Press.

Fox, Renee C. 2004. "Observations and Reflections of a Perpetual Fieldworker." *The ANNALS of the American Academy of Political and Social Science* 595 (1): 309–26.

Frank, A. W. 2000. "The Standpoint of Storyteller." *Qualitative Health Research* 10 (3): 354–65.

Geertz, Clifford. 1973. *The Interpretation of Cultures: Selected Essays*. New York: Basic Books.

———. 1988. *Works and Lives: The Anthropologist as Author*. Stanford, CA: Stanford University Press.

Gergen, Kenneth J., and Mary M. Gergen. 1983. "Narratives of the Self." In *Studies in Social Identity*, edited by Theodore R. Sarbin and Karl E. Scheibe, 254–73. New York: Praeger.

Hoey, Brian A. 2005. "From Pi to Pie: Moral Narratives of Noneconomic Migration and Starting Over in the Postindustrial Midwest." *Journal of Contemporary Ethnography* 34 (5): 586–624.

———. 2014. *Opting for Elsewhere: Lifestyle Migration in the American Middle Class.* Nashville, TN: Vanderbilt University Press.

Hoey, Brian A., and Tom Fricke. 2007. "'From Sweet Potatoes to God Almighty': Roy Rappaport on Being a Hedgehog." *American Ethnologist* 34 (3): 581–99.

Kutsche, Paul. 1998. *Field Ethnography: A Manual for Doing Cultural Anthropology.* Upper Saddle River, NJ: Prentice Hall.

Langness, Lewis L., and Geyla Frank. 1981. *Lives: An Anthropological Approach to Biography.* Novato, CA: Chandler & Sharp.

Lassiter, Luke Eric. 2005. *The Chicago Guide to Collaborative Ethnography.* Chicago: University of Chicago Press.

Lassiter, Luke Eric, Brian A. Hoey, and Elizabeth Campbell. 2020. *I'm Afraid of that Water: A Collaborative Ethnography of a West Virginia Water Crisis.* Morgantown, WV: West Virginia University Press.

Malinowski, Bronislaw. 1922. *Argonauts of the Western Pacific: An Account of Native Enterprise and Adventure in the Archipelagoes of Melanesian New Guinea.* New York: Dutton.

———. 1967. *A Diary in the Strict Sense of the Term.* London: Routledge and Kegan Paul.

Miner, Horace. 1956. "Body Ritual Among the Nacirema." *American Anthropologist* 58: 503–7.

Okely, Judith, and Helen Callaway, eds. 1992. *Anthropology and Autobiography.* Abingdon, UK: Taylor & Francis.

Ortiz, Steven M. 2001. "How Interviewing Became Therapy for Wives of Professional Athletes: Learning From a Serendipitous Experience." *Qualitative Inquiry* 7 (2): 192–220.

Pike, Kenneth L. 1954. *Language in Relation to a Unified Theory of the Structure of Human Behavior.* Glendale, CA: Summer Institute of Linguistics.

Powdermaker, Hortense. 1966. *Stranger and Friend: The Way of an Anthropologist.* New York: Norton & Company.

Reed-Danahay, Deborah. 1997. *Auto/ethnography: Rewriting the Self and the Social.* Explorations in Anthropology. Oxford: Berg.

Roorbach, Bill. 1998. *Writing Life Stories.* Cincinnati, OH: Story Press.

Rosaldo, Renato. 1993. *Culture & Truth: The Remaking of Social Analysis.* Boston: Beacon Press.

Ryle, Gilbert. 1971. *Collected Papers* 2. London: Hutchinson.

Rylko-Bauer, Barbara, Merrill Singer, and John Van Willigen. 2006. "Reclaiming Applied Anthropology: Its Past, Present, and Future." *American Anthropologist* 108 (1): 178-190.

Sanjek, Roger. 2014. *Ethnography in Today's World: Color Full before Color Blind.* Philadelphia: University of Pennsylvania Press.

———. 2015. *Mutuality: Anthropology's Changing Terms of Engagement.* Philadelphia: University of Pennsylvania Press.

Solomon, Robert C. 1978. "Emotions and Anthropology: The Logic of Emotional World Views." *Inquiry* 21 (1-4): 181–99.

Stilgoe, John R. 1999. *Outside Lies Magic: Regaining History and Awareness in Everyday Places.* New York: Walker and Co.

Tedlock, Barbara. 1991. "From Participant Observation to the Observation of Participation: The Emergence of Narrative Ethnography." *Journal of Anthropological Research* 47 (1): 69–94.

van Maanen, John. 1988. *Tales of the Field: On Writing Ethnography.* Chicago: University of Chicago Press.

Yow, Valerie Raleigh. 2005. *Recording Oral History: A Guide for the Humanities and Social Sciences.* 2nd ed. Walnut Creek, CA: AltaMira Press.

Global Health at the Local Level:
Innovative Approaches for Preventing HIV/AIDS Among Adolescent Girls in Botswana with Evidence from an Evaluation Study on Perceptions of Cross Generational Sex and *Edutainment* Strategies

Rebecca L. Upton

Introduction

In Botswana, cross-generational sex (CGS) accounts for a disparity in incidence and prevalence rates of HIV infection between young men and women in the country. Ministry of Health quantitative data and ethnographic research indicate that almost one third of college-aged girls in urban cities had high-risk sex with a partner over ten years older in the past year. Described as "Mma 14s" (in the past this was often translated as "mothers at age 14" or "women at 14") these girls are caught between cultural imperatives that emphasize the "traditional" and global consumption and goals of being a "modern" person. Rates of incidence and prevalence of HIV infection for young women of that age are considerably higher for women despite active education and awareness programs targeted toward the reduction of CGS. Increasingly, global health initiatives have placed emphasis on gender issues in the construction of efficacious, culturally competent prevention strategies but have yet to truly examine how local initiatives (and interpretations) of health messages can facilitate these goals in the twenty-first century.

This chapter describes how a local initiative, *Makgabaneng*, a very popular, long-running radio serial drama, has helped to raise awareness and increase education across the country about CGS. The show, a product of grassroots development and culturally competent strategies, has helped empower young girls as well as community members in their efforts to ameliorate some of the disparities in HIV infection. This approach has had positive outcomes for girls living in urban contexts and from both low and high socio-economic backgrounds, indicating a shift in awareness that transcends assumptions about socioeconomic status (SES) and empowerment. In this chapter, I demonstrate how ethnographically-driven research at the local level helped to inform better strategies for intervention in what has come to be seen as an increasingly problematic aspect of the global epidemic. I suggest that a *reconsideration* of and *reinvestment* in more grassroots and culturally logical messages can help move this phase of HIV and AIDS prevention forward and have a positive impact beyond urban to more rural parts of Botswana.

Context and Drivers of Cross-Generational Sex in Botswana

Studies in different parts of Sub-Saharan Africa indicate that young women aged 15 to 24 are three times more likely to be infected with HIV than males of the same age (cf. Sutherland 2014). The disparity in levels of HIV infection, especially in countries in Sub-Saharan Africa, is of great concern, particularly given the relative success of HIV and AIDS education, prevention, and treatment programs over the past several decades. One explanation for this disparity in infections is age inequality in sexual relationships between older men and young women and the cultural norms and gendered obligations that drive sexual behavior. Older men have higher rates of HIV than young men and the relationships with older men limit young women's power to negotiate safer sex, particularly because there is often exchange of money or gifts for sex. In Botswana, this has meant a new focus and concerted efforts to discourage multiple concurrent partnerships and reduce the "sugar daddy" appeal through the use of various media campaigns and health promotion strategies.[1] In addition, the socioeconomic and power imbalances inherent in cross generational and transactional sexual relationships put young women at high risk of unintended pregnancy and sexually transmitted infections including HIV.

As I have written elsewhere (Upton 2001, 2010, 2015), fertility and pregnancy desires have long been drivers of the HIV and AIDS epidemic in this part of the continent. For many young Tswana women today, however, particularly those in urban areas, these cultural desires have shifted. Just a few years ago, Tirelo, a young college student at the University of Botswana said to me as he lamented his lack of a girlfriend,

> My aunties, my sister, everyone back in my home village asks me all of the time if I have a girlfriend . . . but I tell them that women these days just want the three C's . . . cash, clothes and cell-phones. I can't give them any of that, I'm a student too . . . but those guys outside the gates [of the University grounds], those old men, they can give them all that, they are "big men,"[2] they make it easy for the girls to want to go with them because they can give them everything that they want.

The concept of a "sugar daddy" is not new, and in Botswana, as in many contexts, cross-generational sex among older men and young girls is driven by the need to fulfill wants, as Mpho, a friend of Tirelo's said, for "lipstick, handbags, nail varnish to sweets, chocolates, clothes," and other luxury items. It is sometimes motivated by the hope to get married to a good, already reliable and stable person who, as Sutherland (2014) suggests, in most economic situations in the continent, are characteristics of men of higher ages and social status. In Botswana, as I have argued, while establishing one's fertility has long been considered (for both men and women) a sign of adulthood and indicative of being a productive (as reproductive) member of society, this more recent ethnographic research among college-aged youth suggests that while the three "Cs" may be important, times have changed. As Tirelo put it, "there just isn't a fourth C, there is no child in the picture for those ladies, that is not what is important to them, maybe in the rural villages, but not women here in Gaborone." What has become important at the *local* level and the significant cultural driver of cross-generational sex, is the emphasis that many place on economic benefits that derive from multiple and intergenerational intimate partnerships. As several scholars in Botswana note, "men and women who willingly have intergenerational sexual relationships may feel young and develop very high self-esteem" as a result of these partnerships (Raditloaneng and Molosi 2014, 39) and contributes to a sense of well-being, self-worth, and attractiveness that is culturally sanctioned and perhaps even expected (cf. Mookodi, Ntshebe, and Taylor 2004; Oyediran, Odutolu, and Atobatele 2011).

CGS, HIV, and AIDS in Contemporary Botswana

In Botswana, the association between cross-generational sex, unsafe behaviors, and HIV risk makes the phenomenon a priority concern. While education and awareness, as well as a tremendous amount of international attention and funding to control the epidemic, has long been a part of life in Botswana, HIV incidence and prevalence rates remain higher than expected. In addition, data from the 2014 UNAIDS Gap Report clearly indicate that in much of Botswana, young women continue to bear the brunt of the AIDS epidemic. HIV prevalence among young women aged 15 to 19 is 4.8 percent compared to 2.3 percent among men. In the 20-to-24-year age group, women's prevalence was 6.3 percent compared to 2.4 percent among men. While there are 320,000 people living with HIV and AIDS (PLWHA) in Botswana and an overall prevalence rate of 21.9 percent with 69 percent of the population on ARV (anti-retroviral therapy), this is a considerable drop in overall incidence and prevalence rates over the past two decades, and life expectancy has begun an upward trend. Prevalence among men above 30 years or more peaks at 9.3 percent. Nevertheless, it is widely believed that sex among young women (15 to 24) and men who are ten years or more older is to some extent the cause of the disparity between young women and young men. The Botswana Demographic Health Survey and BAIS III (2010) showed that one in ten young women had sex with a man ten or more years older.

In other parts of the continent, similar findings occur. Ntozi et al. (2003) considered this issue in Uganda over a decade ago. Uganda has long been considered a "success story" in combatting the HIV/AIDS epidemic and for encountering many of these epidemic-related outcomes far earlier than other African countries. They found that the economic conditions of most families have affected the potential of parents to meet the growing demands of their children in a competitive environment (similar to this study in Gaborone, the urban capital of Botswana and site of the national University of Botswana). Thus, the socioeconomic pressures put young women in situations of sexual relationships with men who are perceived to be financially secure.

In addition to the socioeconomic drivers of risky sexual behaviors, older men often express a desire for sexual partnerships with young women, in part because they are believed to be free of HIV and AIDS infection, at least in the more recent decade. In Botswana, campaigns for an "AIDS-free generation" are far more realistic than ever, given the efficacy of ARV therapies and the cultural resilience of fertility outcomes as definitive of individual success and identity, particularly in more rural parts of the country. Now that HIV and

AIDS are seen as more chronic and less fatal conditions, the need for locally-driven and effective approaches to ameliorating CGS and the increasing STI rates in the country have come under public health scrutiny. While much is known about the hazards of cross-generational sex, the effects of existing interventions, particularly in those more rural areas, remain largely unknown.

Given the disproportionate rates of HIV among young women in Botswana as compared to older male counterparts, continued efforts are needed to better understand that the effect of interventions against cross-generational sex and develop evidence-based approaches. While this project was not the first to examine "edutainment" approaches (others have investigated this and a range of popular media designed to engage youth with positive messages and the reduction of stigma) to health promotion in Botswana, it offers a careful re-examination of one approach and suggests its potential use and impact in more underserved parts of the population. Specifically, the overall aim of this study, and one congruent with the aims of this volume, was to determine how interventions with respect to cross-generational sex influenced a change of behavior among young women in tertiary schools (the University of Botswana or teaching colleges in and near the capital city of Gaborone). The study sought to test the hypotheses that young women from low economic status families are more likely to engage in cross generational sex than young women from high economic status families and that young women who are exposed to media campaigns against cross generational sex are less likely to engage in cross generational sex in general. In presenting this work, grounded in ethnographic approaches to evaluation of edutainment strategies, I hope to demonstrate the need to connect local, cultural interpretations to global messages in order to better evaluate the efficacy of public health practices.

The Study Population: Mma 14s and "Mr. Price"

Beginning in 2010, I extensively interviewed twenty-five college-aged women living in Gaborone about their perceptions of gender in the twenty-first century and whether they felt that being an "urban" or "city person" versus living in their home village affected those perceptions. Using qualitative methods and ethnographic practice, I spent a year documenting women's lives in urban Botswana and considering the effects of globalization on bodies and beliefs. In different places, I write about the paradox for many of these young women in terms of concepts of "health; " that globalization and shifts in concepts of beauty, "fatness," and well-being are conflated and confounded with contemporary understandings of the HIV and AIDS epidemic (cf. Upton 2010, 2016). In that work and subsequent research in Botswana, it is clear that whether young adults envision themselves as urban or rural persons at present, they *fundamentally* conceive of themselves as being connected to others across global boundaries, a core theme of this volume as well. Cell phones, videos, television, and social media have facilitated the spread of knowledge and mediate messages in local and global contexts.

In this study, a more focused and follow-up project conducted in 2011 and 2012 for a period of eight months, I asked young women (using individual ethnographic interviews as well as a series of five focus groups formed as a result of snowball sampling from the first project) who were self-reported heavy users of social media and consumers of internet entertainment to respond to open-ended interviews about particular kinds of messages about CGS. Specifically, I asked an additional twenty-five women between the ages of 19 and 25 years of age who were living in Gaborone, Botswana about their perceptions of CGS. Central to the interview instrument was a discussion of the cultural category of a "Mma 14" and how this may have changed over the past several years. All study participants knew and talked about how young women were often seen as "look-ing for a man" or "looking for a sugar daddy" as teenagers, but all were also aware that most young people today did not actively seek pregnancy and motherhood as an initial outcome or as a driver of CGS.

Rather, the stigma of being a "Mma 14" (a mother at age 14) is now *less* about fertility and *more* about financial benefits. As one young woman in a focus group told me, "you definitely want nice things, to be able to buy nice clothes and to buy air time [for cell phones], you want to go into Mr. Price, not just stand outside and look in the window." Others in the focus group nodded in agreement, citing upscale shops (such as the home goods store "Mr. Price" and others like Woolworth's) as desirable. Several even equated the phrase "Mr. Price" with the men who could provide financial benefits themselves. As Daisy and Sethunya, two college-aged friends of Mpho and Tirelo both observed, "city life" is what everyone wants, a comfortable and "globally driven" lifestyle. As Sethunya put it, "girls want to be with Mr. Price because he can *afford* Mr. Price, he can get you things in the mall, he can get you things here in Gabs [Gaborone], the things that everyone wants, he can give you the life we see on TV, and hav-ing a sugar daddy just isn't the problem that our parents, our teachers here at University, adults, think it is." Clearly, being a cosmopolitan and financially comfortable person has its advantages, and for many young women in particular a local strategy for success in these areas is through culturally sanctioned cross-generational sex.

Makgabaneng: An Edutainment Approach

Makgabaneng drama was launched in August 2001. It was the first radio serial drama in Botswana and continues to this day. As early as 2003, the National AIDS Coordinating Agency in Botswana (NACA) increased its surveillance and strategizing within the country to combat the HIV and AIDS epidemic, and one member of the organization called for the implementation of "a wide array of preventive and curative strategies to bring [HIV-infection] to a halt" (Fidzani 2003, 3 in Cole 2011). In tracing the rise of multi-pronged approaches to the epidemic, Cole writes that "radio serial dramas occupy an integral role in public education campaigns" (2011) and suggests in her own analysis of edutainment strategies in this context that *Makgabaneng* offers one of the best examples of grassroots approaches to behavior change.

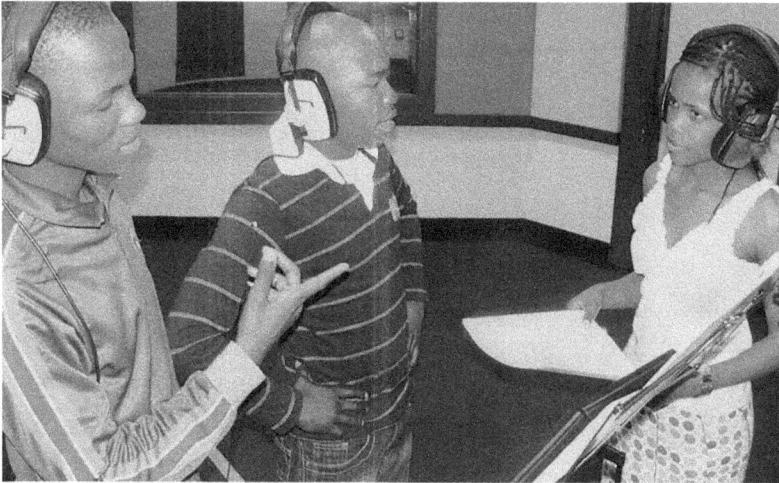

The *Makgabaneng* recording studio (Photo courtesy of *Makgabaneng* [NGO], Gaborone, Botswana)

Makgabaneng is one of the many preventive strategies that have been formed in Botswana over the past ten years. It uses HIV/AIDS health education and behavioral change programs to transform perceptions of HIV and AIDS in the country. Maungo Mooki believes *Makgabaneng* serves as a "gateway to behavioral change" that can make considerable contributions to Botswana's HIV/AIDS epidemic (Cole 2011). While efforts to ameliorate, address, and abolish HIV/AIDS from the country have been ongoing for the past two decades, recent discourse and focus on locally-driven initiatives has grown. Specifically, as the fiftieth anniversary of the nation's independence occurred in 2016, much of the government-sponsored research and propaganda emphasized the potential for Botswana to be "HIV/ AIDS Free" in the near future.[3] Based on the program's various accomplishments and successes, members of the *Makgabaneng* staff had long been convinced that the "trajectory" of the serial drama was "endless" (cf. Cole's research on this and based upon extensive interviews with the actors/staff themselves) and that the drama was slated to continue until "the war on HIV/AIDS in Botswana is won" (Tembo 2003). As Cole describes it, *Makgabaneng* is a "behavior change SeTswana-language edutainment radio serial drama designed to support the nation's HIV prevention and mitigation goals" (2011, p.144). The serial targets 10-to-49-year-old BaTswana and combines the drama with community-based reinforcement activities to encourage safer HIV related behaviors (such as delaying initiation of sex, being faithful, accessing services and providing support to people living with HIV/AIDS). *Makgabaneng* uses the Global Reproductive Health Communication Strategy Framework: Modeling and Reinforcement to Combat HIV/AIDS (MARCH), which has been developed by CDC's Division of Reproductive Health. In the sections that follow, I illustrate how relevant themes that emerged in conversation supported and may help shape the efficacy of ongoing (and even future) local health strategies such as this.

Evaluating the Efficacy of Health Communication Strategies

Emergent and Relevant Themes in Makgabaneng

In this section, I highlight several examples that reflect general responses to and usage of the material found in *Makgabaneng* that emerged during the focus group and ethnographic interviewing I conducted. During interviews and focus groups about the series, several specific themes emerged in response to questions about efficacy of the series and relevance to everyday life. Many respondents noted that themes about partner violence and CGS were connected and were all the more relevant depending upon where in the country people were listening. Many argued that while CGS might be higher in the cities and urban areas, those who "needed to know about those issues" would be located in the more rural and northern parts of the country. Others argued that initially *Makgabaneng* was defined broadly and could appeal (and be relevant) to all, but that plot lines had initially been more generally about the impact of HIV/AIDS on everyday lives. Many noted that more *recent* story lines involved CGS, globalization, and issues beyond just the epidemic, however, and suggested that in fact *Makgabaneng* was a fair reflection of both how "Tswana people live" and recent awareness around the country of intimate or gender-based violence (GBV) as a global issue.

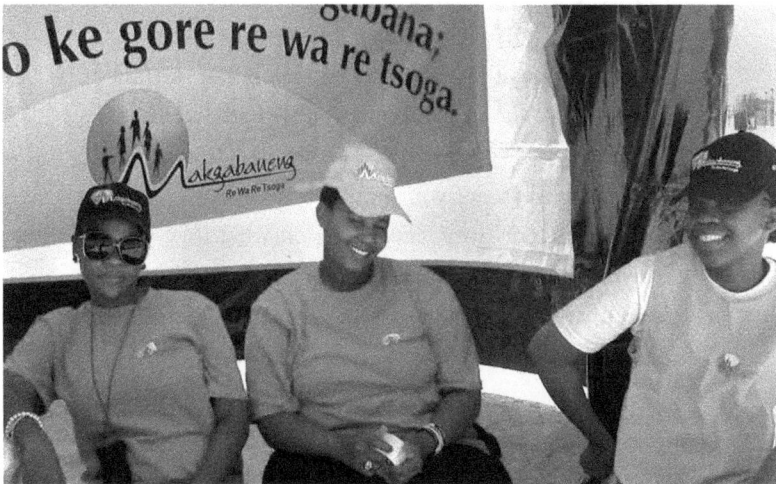

A *Makgabaneng*-sponsored health fair in the village of Letlhakeng, Botswana (Photo courtesy of *Makgabaneng* [NGO], Gaborone, Botswana)

HIV/AIDS

Like much of the rest of the education and prevention strategies that have been ubiquitous throughout the country over the past few decades, *Makgabaneng* has emphasized individual agency and the promotion of behavior change. While early prevention messages reflected more global emphases on the ABCs of prevention (Abstain, Be Faithful and Condomise), messages in many of the *Makgabaneng* episodes address the need for HIV testing. In this study, participants mentioned repeatedly that the show must emphasize more than just testing in order to stay relevant and have an impact. As Letsatsi, a 21-year-old first-year student at the University of Botswana, described it,

> My generation, the college students you see around here and youth in Gaborone ... we've grown up with HIV and AIDS, it's like the air we breathe, we are so used to knowing, hearing, learning about it. AIDS is nothing new for us so we're used to testing. [laughs] I think every event when we were kids gave away a t-shirt or bag that encouraged people to get tested, so it's almost not even something to think about, you know you will get tested, you know people are and that it's probably okay to ask about status. [laughs] Is everyone going to tell you the truth? That's a different story, depending on what they want, what you want, but it's not a taboo to ask about testing or to encourage it, that's a real change from my parents and when the epidemic first came to our country.

When asked about *Makgabaneng* specifically Letsatsi said,

> They definitely need to keep doing more to be in touch with younger generations, they reflect what people are doing and thinking about in terms of HIV but life is moving faster ... so they need to pay attention even more

to the issues of violence, to what's happening on campus these days with the sugar daddies. One of my first professors on campus, she was telling me that she wanted to close the University gates and make it impossible for those old guys to come around looking for us [young female students] . . . [laughs] I don't think that will happen, they have the guard at the gates, but people come and go all of the time, you can walk out and in and nobody wants to have it be a prison just to prevent the sugar daddies. Some of my friends, yes, they are in those kinds of relationships, it's not good, because you have to put up with a lot, sometimes the men are greedy and want you all the time and it takes time away from studies. But the money is nice. Yes, the shows on the radio need to incorporate some more of those stories.

In fact, Letsatsi and her friends (some of whom admitted to being in a CGS relationship and were willing to speak with me) all described how some evenings, if they were listening to the show or talking about it, they actually came up with plots and episodes that they thought would be appealing. I asked them if they had ever written in to the *Makgabaneng* staff with their suggestions, and while they had not, the idea held appeal and suggested one avenue for improving the resonance of the show for future audiences.

While HIV and AIDS have now long been a part of the everyday life of many young BaTswana, it was clear in this study that other, locally relevant factors intersect in the lives of young people. Specifically, ideas of intimate violence and the various outcomes of being a part of a cross-generational sexual partnership are both real and in need of discussion. An overwhelming majority of respondents in my study spoke about their own as well a general Tswana cultural familiarity with HIV and AIDS (it is not uncommon today to hear people talk about having "AIDS fatigue," a social exhaustion from hearing about the disease for years that runs the risk of alienating people from seeking health care) and pointed to the new issues at hand for young people. If the three "Cs" that Tirelo and his friends spoke about no longer include "children" and fertility concerns to the same degree they once did for their parents, it is all the more important to look at other issues that are salient and affect risk of STIs and HIV.

Gender-Based Violence

Attention to gender-based violence has increased over the past decade in Botswana. Policies and productions such as *Makgabaneng* began to emphasize (and recognize) the need to bring men into conversations about HIV/AIDS prevention. A key collection of essays by local academics and advocates in Botswana makes clear that male involvement in research and HIV and AIDS programming is essential for any future efficacy in policy and public health (cf. Maundeni et al. 2009). Lekoko suggests that patriarchal systems in Tswana culture have meant that social tolerance of multiple sexual partners and intimate violence and coercion in relationships have directly contributed to the failure of many HIV and AIDS prevention programs over the past two decades (in Maundeni et al. 2009, 91).

In this project, study participants were asked to explain several Tswana proverbs in the context of health; specifically, the expressions, "monna selepe o a amogwana" (a man is like an axe in demand, going from one to another) and "monna poo ga a agelwe mosako" (bulls cannot be contained to a single corral). Most participants talked about these expressions in terms of the license they give to men in relationships, either in terms of power or actual violence against women. Kabo, a 23-year-old male student living in the capital city of Gaborone, described how,

> When we were children and we would go visit relatives at the cattle post or my mother's home village [more rural parts of the country], people would always act like the boys were the little men already . . . we thought it was great but as you grow you have to think about what the messages are that boys are getting . . . sometimes there were real conflicts in the messages at home versus what you learn in school or on TV, on the radio and from your girl friends too [laughs] like there is no way that you were going to be a "big person" or a "big man" with your girl friends who you grew up with.

Kabo is a peer counselor at his agriculture college and a mentor for youth and he continued,

> The expressions, those proverbs, they reinforce the negative messages about men. Yes, yes, about men . . . that men can and maybe even should do these things to women in order to be respected. It is a dangerous path to be told that men should have many partners . . . or that they can hit them . . . those are messages that today's youth are more skeptical about. Multiple partners these days, that's something that women are doing more . . . nobody is blaming them but it is more attractive to get something from older men than younger ones and many will tell you it is empowering, they are not being beaten, they are beating the men at their own game.

It was significant to hear from numerous participants in this study that young women, those who considered themselves fans of *Makgabaneng* and who identified as those involved in multiple or cross-generational relationships, saw themselves as "close to" some of the characters on the show. While others have noted the resonance that audience members had with certain regular characters on the show in positive ways (cf. Lovell et al. 2007)—thinking about the possibility of HIV exposure, for example—it was clear in this research that many women felt that they were "smarter" than the characters. For example, Osi, a 24-year-old student told me that "many of the show's characters are discussing real things, real problems, but we have different ones, we're smarter about how to deal with sugar daddies and to still get everything from them, except HIV." Like Peirce (2011), it seems clear that through ethnographic investigation of themes and audience acceptance of *Makgabaneng*, there are some gaps when it comes to adequate discussion of violence and of the actual empowerment of women and CGS, areas often overlooked by larger global health emphases and programming on HIV and AIDS. As others in this volume suggest, here we see the value of alternatives to the status quo and the role of individuals in crafting different and potentially more efficacious approaches to social problems such as HIV/AIDS.

Cross-Generational Sex

When asked whether they had cross-generational sex or knew of someone who had, all of the participants in each focus group responded positively. But many respondents in this evaluation study talked about how actual awareness of CGS had increased and that interventions and peer pressure not to engage in multiple or cross-generational sex was growing. Participants in this evaluation were quick to point out that intervening and telling one's peers not to engage in CGS was positively valued. Additionally, while not a part of early *Makgabaneng* plot lines, most felt that CGS was one of the more profoundly important public health problems for BaTswana today. As Mmamelodi, a 34-year-old mother of three, put it, "this is how young women, girls of today, will see their futures. I'm working hard so that my girls do not think that they should be falling for these old men." She continued, "being a Mma 14 for girls a generation ago was okay because having children young was still valued, but now that label, it indicates being with one of these older men, these married men." A recent study builds upon and echoes what Mmamelodi told me, concluding that young girls and women in more rural areas, those without as much education and those seeking financial prestige, were more likely to engage in CGS (Sutherland, 2014).

In this research, participants talked about how interventions such as *Makgabaneng*, those that are seen as long-standing, respected and resonant, can and do have an impact upon decisions to enter a CGS relationship. For many participants, and those who described themselves as "long-time listeners" such as Letsatsi described above, CGS was considered the most pressing and relevant issue. Mpho, a friend of Letsatsi's and a woman who had had several CGS relationships, said the following in a focus group,

> There are a lot of billboards telling us to say no to sugar daddies, the ones that we probably all know are the ones, "cross generational sex stops with you," and to "respect yourself, the gifts aren't worth it" . . . I think the recent one that asks "would you let this man be with your teenage daughter, so why are you with him?" and is geared toward much more community responsibility . . . I understand all that and those are good messages, but for myself I wanted to be better off, these men offer nice things, some security, and these days nobody worries as much about getting sick.

Mpho's explanation of CGS was arguably not about the risk of contracting HIV or STIs, because in an ironic twist of public health, the success of prevention messaging over the years and the advent of ARV (anti-retroviral therapies) means that living with HIV and AIDS is not a death sentence. The positive outcomes associated with CGS can now far outweigh the stigma or perceived danger of such relationships. As Itumeleng, an acquaintance of Mpho and Letsatsi and a member of the same focus group in which Mpho made the statement above, said,

> Billboards, radio shows, television, school programs, all of this has been going on our whole lives and we are aware . . . we are aware of HIV and AIDS and STIs and nobody wants to get those diseases but we also know they are treatable, the government will pay for your care and you can live a healthy life. All those shows, they focus on testing, making the male partners involved and what they should focus on is that we are still at risk. Those diseases are manageable, but people think they will live forever and they want to live in the moment, live nicely, especially when we are all young and in school, you have nothing so you are tempted to find a sugar daddy, be taken care of.

When asked about *Makgabaneng* in particular, Itumeleng observed that while more could be done on the show about CGS, it was a good medium. As she put it, "people pay attention to what the show says and what happens to the characters, I've even written to them to say what I think about certain stories and lives that influence me, I could be those characters and that makes a difference." Itumeleng, Mpho and Letsatsi all reiterated that the messages in *Makgabaneng* made a difference in their lives because the issues felt "local" and "like they could be happening" to all of them in contrast to the ubiquitous (albeit arguably successful for the most part) messages they have received about HIV and AIDS throughout their young lives.

Discussion—the Relevance of the Local for the Global

Cole (2011) writes about the efficacy of *Makgabaneng* in terms of modeling positive behavioral change and boosting self-efficacy in its strategies for reduction of HIV/AIDS over the years. Specifically, and as was clear in my own evaluation study using the serial, this program offers a sound, culturally relevant and realistic set of scenarios that reinforced positive change. Clearly, too, having personalized the problem of HIV/AIDS means that audience members, wherever they are located, can share in the "imagined community" (cf. Anderson 1983) of healthier, positive, and supportive environments across the country. Drawing upon the serial and its scripts over the years has seemingly lessened the stereotypes as to who has HIV/AIDS, who is more prone to intimate violence, and, more recently, who might be at risk for negative outcomes associated with CGS. *Makgabaneng* stories lessen stigma and create connections across communities.

In a self-evaluation and ongoing critique of the serial, *Makgabaneng* staff have documented how effective "letter writing strategies" have been in the efforts to keep content current and relevant. Specifically, fans of the show and the community writ large are periodically welcomed to submit letters in response to questions about their favorite episodes, characters, or situations. Letters to the radio show reveal that fans have, in fact, internalized many of the messages as related to HIV/AIDS (cf. Cole's discussion of an episode entitled, "Masego and Cecilia," 2011) and have created a dialectic between the fans and the broader social issues that are embodied in the narratives of the show. Local populations (and there were overwhelmingly large responses from women and those in rural communities) felt and still feel connected to broader conversations about what it means to be informed, in conversation with and affected by more globally "visible" (or in this case perhaps "louder") messages about HIV/AIDS and other public health threats.

A listening and discussion group (LDG) in the village of Tutume, Botswana. (Photo courtesy of *Makgabaneng* [NGO], Gaborone, Botswana)

Two things are clear in assessing the efficacy of *Makgabaneng* as a form of edutainment in Botswana: One is that the duration, the length of time that people listened to and felt connected by the shifting stories over the years, has had an impact on behaviors—even as the HIV/AIDS threats have changed over the years (CGS was not something that people felt "existed" prior to the last five years, for example) suggesting that like ethnography, long-term participation in a local context can actually change the global public health problem.

Second, this assessment points to the rise of "radio role models," a context in which technology and mobile phone use and, in particular, Twitter have strong footholds for a majority of the population, both rural and urban alike. Despite social media, radio role models, characters who individuals imagine to be like themselves, can act as mediators between online and lived experiences. Specifically, radio role models occupy a kind of "imagined community" in which their voices, their experiences, and the outcomes of their behaviors are subject to interpretation by those in the less-virtual world. Their voices are relevant, however, as the local interpretations are always and inherently connected to a constellation of global health concerns. Even in the most remote part of northern Botswana, individuals talking about *Makgabaneng* think of themselves as "connected" in the conversation about HIV/AIDS, CGS, and GBV.

Conclusion

In 2007, Carter et al. wrote that in Botswana, "efforts to reduce the risks associated with concurrency and multiple partnerships are hindered further by the lack of examples and *evaluations of interventions* that effectively target partner reduction and faithfulness" (p. 829, emphasis added). Now, almost a decade later, it is clear that with added ethnographic research, the complexity of Tswana social, economic, and gendered lives reveals that these efforts must take into account the local constructions of health or priorities about sex and reproduction. Similarly, with respect to this study of cross-generational sex and a particular intervention strategy, the *Makgabaneng* radio drama, understanding local concepts will always lead to improved health outcomes at a global level. Reclaiming anthropological best practices that ground our understanding of "what makes sense" in local terms will logically and practically lead to stronger health programming and more efficacious interventions for all. Evaluation of locally produced and inspired edutainment strategies offer but one among many examples of those practices and the power of the ethnographic endeavor. From central themes of this volume, such as the valence of cultural resilience and the very real actions of individuals within communities to effect change, *Makgabaneng* offers a useful lens to consider what we mean by empowerment and activism at the local level. Tswana individuals, like those in other chapters in this volume, illustrate through their actions both cultural resistance as well as adaptability and the reshaping of health-related policy from the perspective of those most affected. Ultimately, *Makgabaneng* becomes a way in which ethnographers can see how individuals really *see* themselves through the craft and consumption of contemporary media.

NOTES

1. The *o icheke* campaign, or "check yourself" campaign is one recent example of a media health promotion strategy that was designed to reduce the appeal of CGS and multiple sexual partners. Billboards for example, with the *o icheke* slogan and reminders to check who was in one's sexual network were ubiquitous for the past several years throughout the capital city of Gaborone and well-traveled roads across Botswana.
2. Historically a term to describe an individual in a Tswana community with a good deal of political power, economic wealth or social prestige.
3. Vision 2016 is a governmental plan to obliterate HIV/AIDS in Botswana. The details of this program can be found in *Towards an AIDS-Free Generation: Botswana Human Development Report 2000—The Popular Version* (UNDP 2001).

WORKS CITED

Anderson, Benedict. 1983. *Imagined Communities: Reflections on the Origin and Spread of Nationalism*. London: Verso.

Barz, Gregory and Judah Cohen, eds. 2011. *The Culture of AIDS in Africa: Hope and Healing Through Music and the Arts*. Oxford University Press.

Carter, Marion W., Joan Marie Kraft, Todd Koppenhaver, Christine Galavotti, Thierry H. Roels, Peter H. Kilmarx, and Boga Fidzani. 2007. "'Bull Cannot be Contained in a Single Kraal': Concurrent Sexual Partnerships in Botswana." *AIDS and Behaviour* 11: 822.

Cole, Abimbola. 2011. "Contemporary Uses of the Musical Arts in Botswana's HIV/AIDS Health Education Initiatives." In *The Culture of AIDS in Africa*, edited by Gregory Barz and Judah M. Cohan, 144–157. Oxford: Oxford University Press.

Fidzani, Boga. 2003. "HIV/AIDS Preventative Behavior in Botswana: Trends and Determinants at the Turn of the 21st Century." Ph.D. diss. University of Southern California.

Lovell, Camille Collins, Katina A. Pappas-DeLuca, Anne K. Sebert Kuhlmann, Todd Koppenhaver, Sandra Kong, Maungo Mooki, and Christine Galavotti. 2007. "'One Day I Might Find Myself HIV-Positive Like Her': Audience Involvement and Identification with Role Models in an Entertainment-Education Radio Drama in Botswana." *International Quarterly Community Health Education* 28 (3), 181–200.

Maundeni, T., B. Osei-Hwedie, E. P. Mukamaambo, and P. Ntseane, eds. 2009. *Male Involvement in Sexual and Reproductive Health: Prevention of Violence and HIV/AIDS in Botswana*. Cape Town: Made Plain Communications.

Mookodi, Godisang, Oleosi Ntshebe, and Ian Taylor. 2004. "Botswana." In *The Continuum Complete International Encyclopedia of Sexuality*, edited by R.F. Noonan and R. Noonan, 89–97. New York: Continuum.

Ntozi, James P. M., Innocent Mulindwa Najjumba, Fred Ahimbisibwe, Natal Ayiga, Jonathan Odwee. 2003. "Has the HIV/AIDS Epidemic Changed Sexual Behaviour of High Risk Groups in Uganda?" *African Health Sciences* 3: 107–116.

Oyediran, K. A., O. Odutolu, and A. O. Atobatele. 2011. "Intergenerational Sexual Relationship in Nigeria: Implications for Negotiating Safe Sexual Practices." In *Social and Psychological Aspects of HIV/AIDS and their Ramifications*, edited by Gobopamang Letamo, 49–72. London: InTech.

Peirce, Meghan. 2011. "Botswana's Makgabaneng: An Audience Reception Study of an Edutainment Drama." Unpublished Ph.D. diss. Scripps College of Communication of Ohio University.

Raditloaneng, Wapula N. and Keneilwe Molosoi. 2014. "A Gendered View of Intergenerational Sex, and Materialism in Predisposition to HIV/AIDS: Implications for Adult Higher Education in Botswana." *Journal of Research in Peace, Gender and Development*. 4 (3): 38–47.

Sutherland, Marcia E. 2014. "Innovative Approaches for Preventing HIV among Adolescent Girls in Uganda: Evidence from an Evaluation Study on Anti Cross Generation Sex in Secondary Schools." *Journal of HIV/AIDS & Infectious Diseases*. 2 (302): 1–4.

Tembo, Prisca, Christine Galavotti, Todd Koppenhaver, Katina Pappas-DeLuca, and Peter Kilmarx. 2003. "'Dear Makgabaneng': An Analysis of Letters Received in Response to an HIV/AIDS Behavior Change Radio Drama." Unpublished presentation at the National HIV/AIDS Research and Other Related Infectious Diseases Conference, December 8.

UNAIDS. 2014. "The Gap Report." http://files.unaids.org/en/media/unaids/contentassets/documents/unaidspublication/2014/UNAIDS_Gap_report_en.pdf

Upton, Rebecca L. 2001. "Infertility Makes You Invisible: Gender, Health and the Negotiation of Childbearing in Northern Botswana." *Journal of Southern African Studies*. 27 (2): 349–362.

———. 2010. "Promising the Permanent Condom: Fertility Fears and Fatal Outcomes as a Result of Voluntary Adult Male Circumcision in HIV/AIDS Botswana." *PULA: Journal of Research in Botswana*. 24 (1): 101–117.

———. 2015. "HIV Prevention, Infertility and Concordance in Partner Selection Among Couples Living with HIV/AIDS in Rural and Peri-Urban Contexts in Botswana." *Journal of AIDS and Clinical Research* 6: 526. doi:10.4172/2155-6113.1000526

———. 2016. "Fat Eggs and Fit Bodies." *Contexts*. Journal of the American Sociological Association. 15 (4): 24–29.

Flipping the Microscope:
Peer Education, Race, and Fieldwork in a South African Travel Course

Scott London and Kristen Klaaren

Introduction

This chapter explores the experience of a group of young South African university students who served as peer educators on an American January-term travel course to Johannesburg. This peer education program was designed to create an experiential learning opportunity for American students, and we were surprised to discover the significant impact on the peer educators themselves. Hired to work as "cultural consultants" to help the Americans have an immersive anthropological fieldwork experience, the course structure inadvertently carved out a space in which the relationship was flipped, enabling the peers to benefit in unforeseen ways from their own participant-observation with the students from the United States. Rather than a unilateral learning process emulating conventional fieldwork, the two diverse groups of young adults co-created their own local cultural territory in which they could explore each other's local knowledge concerning race and other topics.

The chief surprise was how much the South Africans valued this opportunity beyond the simple job description they were hired to fill. This unexpected outcome prompted us to investigate how the peer education model benefitted young South Africans, and how these benefits might be expanded. The findings presented here come from open-ended interviews conducted with eight out of twenty of the peer educators who worked with 60 American students over three different travel courses.

The interviews indicate that these young South Africans placed a high value on building personal connections with the Americans students, and that along the way they became keen observers of American culture and custom. The peers were earnest about introducing the students to South Africa, finding the process both exhilarating and exasperating. They relished the opportunity to make new discoveries about their own country, and valued processing their experiences with both the Americans and their fellow peers. The relationships among the diverse peer educators was particularly significant, as most had never before befriended or discussed history and politics with a South African of a different race. This points to the possibilities of using peer education to promote dialogue on issues of race in South Africa.

The interview responses fall roughly into three categories: 1) ethnographic perspectives on American culture and customs, 2) insights into the effectiveness of the peer education model, and 3) reflections on the value of the program for the peer educators themselves. In each instance, issues of race twine around the peers' experiences with the American students and with each other.

International Peer Education as Fieldwork

Short-term international travel courses present a distinctive learning opportunity for students interested in discovering a new culture. Spending time in a foreign country provides opportunities for engaged study unavailable in a classroom back home. Personal encounters with people, sites, and sounds add a rich experiential core to the learning process. But the richness of the experience may depend on skirting a number of pitfalls, not least the limitations of a brief visit framed by tourism. Anthropology professors, in particular, may feel compelled to set the bar low for fostering participant-observation experiences when the standard for ethnographic fieldwork is typically months or years, not weeks. In courses that travel to less industrialized or affluent societies, preoccupation with comfort or safety on the part of students—and a lack of interest on the part of local people in sharing everyday life with transient strangers—may make significant ethnographic encounters unlikely. These were the challenges we had in mind when we decided to experiment with a peer education model. We hoped that bringing American and South African students together might provide a cross-cultural "short-cut," enabling them to establish rapport in a concentrated period and to experience South Africa side-by-side (Klaaren, London, and Klaaren 2006).

Structure of the Peer Education Model and the Travel Course

All the students were enrolled in two introductory-level courses: a cultural anthropology course titled *Gender, Law, and Social Transformation in South Africa* and a social psychology course titled *Race, Privilege, and Social Transformation in South Africa.* During the first week on campus in the United States, the students met six hours per day, two hours for each of the courses and an additional two hours on the history and culture of South Africa. During the following three weeks in South Africa, there was no formal classroom instruction and the two courses were effectively merged. While gender continued to be studied through assignments and activities, race was the dominant topic in formal and informal discussion.

The peer educators met the American students at Wits University the day after arrival in Johannesburg. The daily schedule was heavy, and the peers accompanied the students for all trips, tours, and lectures. The peers were scheduled to accompany the students from nine a.m. to five p.m. but usually elected to spend evenings and days off with them as well. The peer educators saw many of these activities as exciting learning opportunities, some of which were otherwise out of reach for logistical or financial reasons. The peers reported being stimulated by the chance to process these experiences along with the American students, comparing notes, answering questions, engaging in lengthy discussions afterwards over meals or drinks.

In addition to daily field note requirements, the students had several small research assignments that did not have to involve the peer educators but often did, including ethnographic interviews, participant-observation exercises, and a current events project. Students and peers also formed blended groups to participate in topical dialogue groups. Structured activities consisted of almost daily lectures and panels by South African academics and activists, including Constitutional Court Justice Edwin Cameron. A variety of topics included the struggle for equality during the Apartheid era, the South African constitution, gender-based violence, the HIV/AIDS crisis, and LGBTQ issues. Field trips included visits to three townships, the Apartheid Museum, the Constitutional Court, the theatre, and Pilanesberg National Park for a safari.

Unstructured time was cited as particularly valuable by both peers and students, not least because it helped them to process together the sights and sounds they had absorbed, and to decompress after a long day. The bed and breakfast in the Melville neighborhood in Johannesburg and an array of restaurants, bars, and clubs provided abundant leisure spaces. Two of the most memorable events were large dinner parties in the homes of colleagues that turned unexpectedly into group explorations of lived experience under Apartheid, as South Africans of different ages and races shared their stories or those of their parents and grandparents as the American students looked on.

The first set of peer educators were hired through interviews at Wits University in Johannesburg. In subsequent years, hiring was done through referrals, with some peers coming from other universities as well. The peers were paid (from the travel course fees paid by the American students) commensurate with the salary paid to undergraduate research assistants at Wits University, as well as a stipend for food and travel. Hiring was done with an eye toward diversity, and most peer educators identified as black or white, as well as highlighting other identities (for example, some of the peers took pains to share the significance of other identities, such as Zulu or Afrikaner).

Reimagining Ethnography/Reinventing the Local

We argue that the peer education model is valuable for fostering ethnographic encounters and teaching anthropological methods, even though the actual experience of undergraduates on a brief travel course diverges from the work of professional anthropologists in myriad ways. Among these is the fact that the typical trappings of the anthropologist in the field are missing. The intrepid researcher is replaced with the class trip. Instead of the long-term immersion of the individual of one culture into the group life of another, we have two collections of people engaged in shifting subgroups as they roam together through a landscape of class activities. At the same time, this unusual configuration poses some intriguing questions about how we imagine the ethnographic encounter must be, and where it must take place.

We found that bringing together two groups of young people from different cultures into their own joint space creates the possibility of new kinds of cross-cultural learning. Rather than a static trading of facts across a divide, the sharing of knowledge was often chaotic and at times synergistic—discussions of race, for instance, ebbed and flowed over cultural commonalities and differences both within and between groups. Racism and oppression were denied, asserted, and debated amid shifting definitions and cultural assumptions from two sets of national experience. Do such interactions constitute ethnographic fieldwork? What is the meaning of a "field site" if these interactions happen on-the-go, in a mobile space co-created by students from two cultures?

These questions are embedded in challenges dating back decades, posed from within the discipline, to its most iconic image of a lone researcher traveling far in search of knowledge of exotic people (see, e.g., Clifford 1988, Marcus and Fischer 1986, Rosaldo 1989). These challenges have served anthropology well by putting old assumptions under a new light. A key example is the proper role of *informants* and their relationships with ethnographers. As anthropology seeks to take account of the power relations that shape societies and the interactions that constitute them, a top-down, *informant as knowledge commodity* model has become problematic, and relationships based on *dialogue* rather than extraction have become more common. Lassiter (2001) summarizes the turn toward a more "collaborative" and "reciprocal" approach to working with informants as marked by a shift in metaphors from "'reading *over* the shoulders of natives' to 'reading *alongside* natives'" (2001, 138). Paul Rabinow (1977) describes the key role of *friends* in his fieldwork in Morocco, people who taught him about the culture through shared moments of clarity that were nonetheless limited by differences of perspective and imperfect communication. For Rabinow, ethnography is "intersubjective," the result of dialogue between two parties who must continually work to understand each other. Our short travel course model, while a very imperfect reflection of standard anthropological fieldwork, places students from different cultures alongside each other, giving them a chance to befriend one another and to "read" each other's cultures over the din on a noisy bus.

The issue of the *location* in fieldwork has also come under scrutiny, as the standard model of distant travel gives way to a less rigidly territorial conception of where ethnography needs to take place. In the first chapter of their edited volume *Anthropological Locations* (1997), Gupta and Ferguson identify the "contradiction" in a discipline still wed to a methodology that dictates long-term fieldwork in a single location, yet also determined to "give up its old ideas of territorially fixed communities and stable, localized cultures, and to apprehend an interconnected world in which people, objects, and ideas are rapidly shifting and refuse to stay in place" (1997, 4). This challenge to conventional, clearly-bounded field sites enables fieldwork as a method to adapt to new conditions and technologies that reflect a more interconnected and globalized world (see, e.g., Hannerz 2003 on multi-site ethnography, and Modan 2016 on fieldwork using new media). Yet this shift risks a loss of focus on anthropology's distinctive ability to explore the local worlds where most people live. This is perhaps no more apparent than in the realm of "engaged anthropology," in which anthropological methods are put to the task of solving human problems (see Low and Merry 2010). In this instance, painting a portrait of a bounded community of people who share a set of cultural values and interests—even if it is partial and contingent—can be useful, especially if it conveys the understanding that the people themselves are eager to share as active participants in the research. Wagner (this volume), for example, details the benefits of using fieldwork to gather and interpret local knowledge relevant to a power line project in Appalachia. Here, community members themselves train to conduct ethnographic interviews, becoming both subjects and producers of research that empowers local participation in the decision-making process. This form of local engagement, moreover, need not preclude insights from consideration of external processes. Indeed, theorizing about location and fieldwork may point to the ongoing need for pliable definitions that can be tooled with particular projects in mind.

As we moved around the city, this culturally and racially diverse group of students and peers carved out their own shifting terrain through dialogue and shared experience. We believe there is value in describing this in spatial terms because the engagement unfolded in spaces that never felt wholly South African or American, but were rather a reflection of the ongoing "intersubjective" interactions among all these young people. Our research shows that a key result was a sense of engagement and learning on both sides of the equation. In her work on engaged anthropology in Appalachia, Wagner demonstrates how collaboration among community members, student researchers, and anthropologists can foster reciprocity and a mutual feeling of having gained something satisfying and special from the experience. While our course was less problem-driven in an explicitly political sense, the issues of race and racism were a focal point for a lot of closely engaged discussion, from which both groups report gaining a great deal of knowledge and insight.

We are unaware of other research on using peer education as the foundation of an international travel course. But engaged anthropology has formed the backbone of a growing number of travel courses that emphasize research experience and international service learning (see, e.g., Crabtree 2013, Nickols et al. 2013; for a discussion of an international service learning project through the prism of engaged and activist anthropology, see Goldstein 2012). We believe that the peer education model could be easily adapted for travel courses built around service learning projects.

Peer Educators' Ethnographic Perspectives on Americans in South Africa

A primary role of the peer educators was to help to create an experience of doing ethnographic fieldwork in a very brief period of time. Although we did not anticipate how the peers themselves would view their time with the Americans, anthropological fieldwork as a rule carries the potential for a richly reciprocal learning process. It should come as no surprise that the peer educators—intelligent and thoughtful university students self-selected to participate—would be eager to build rapport and learn from their American peers. Their curiosity, fueled by pop culture images and common comparisons between the United States and South Africa, encouraged close engagement with the students. The peers observed closely as the young Americans grappled with culture shock and ethnocentrism, and their response was a mix of compassion and exasperation.

The peers and students were mismatched in more ways than one. Coming from families where their mothers and fathers had little access to higher education under Apartheid, these young South Africans conveyed a tenacious and grateful attitude toward being at university. In contrast, many of the Americans came from privileged and sheltered backgrounds and appeared generally less inclined to take their education seriously. From our perspective, the peers seemed more mature overall, and less parochial in their worldview. One result was that the peer educators typically saw more clearly when the students' behavior became problematic. Johannesburg holds many big city perils for the uninitiated, and the students' privileged assumption of security often led them to resist the peers' seasoned counsel. Describing people who they generally considered good friends, the peers nonetheless made critical note of an array of characteristics that they found in the students. Moments of ethnocentrism and cultural insensitivity live large in their anecdotes.

The peers describe instances of the students' ethnocentric responses with a mix of incredulity and indulgence. Evoking a caricature of Americans at a McDonalds's restaurant in a foreign country, Noma describes students reacting badly to the small portions.

> I remember one of them wanted a McDonald's. "I just want to have McDonald's!" And when she went there, it's like, "Oh my goodness! The size!" You're sitting there and you're thinking, "Well you wanted McDonald's, that's the size we have in South Africa.". . . But, it's just one of those experiences where you get that culture shock and you learn a lot from it. (Noma, black peer educator)

Ndaba speaks often of the students being "independent." Elsewhere in the interview, he suggests that this trait can be positive, but here he links it to arrogance and cultural insensitivity.

> They are very, very independent. They just, they want anything, they just go at it. I want this . . . why must we first have to think is it right? . . . Is it their culture? Is it really offensive if I do this? Also, another thing that I think I picked up, the pride with which they walked. You know you could see from a distance, they walk with such pride. . . . I always thought, maybe it's the Americans, you know all the time they're so independent, you walk like you owned the world. (Ndaba, black peer educator)

The drinking habits of the students were seen as generally problematic among the peers, although most members of both groups consumed alcohol together regularly in the evenings. Americans on travel courses over much of the world revel in lower drinking ages. But the students were seen by the peers as prone to excess, with vulnerability to crime or assault being the primary concern. Toka marvels over the abandon of the students in the evenings at bars and nightclubs.

> I mean they drink to be sloshed, like, you know, they say, oh, what's this expression that they use? They use, there's an expression, like, I know, they want to "pass out." I mean they take shots and have these competitions and they just take shots. And I think, I think at the end of the day, I realize it's . . . sort of the culture. I don't know whether it's American culture or youth culture . . . but I was shocked, you know, the amount of liquor they take in, and how proud they were for doing that. "Jeez, did you see that I was out?!" (Toka, black peer educator)

Several of the peers recalled an activity in which we paired a visit to the high-end Sandton Mall with one to the impoverished urban Alexandra Township just a few miles apart in order to highlight persistent economic inequalities. We were fortunate that day to have a tour guide who wanted to show us where he lived in a hostel in the township. The hostels are infamous for their role in the exploitation of migrant laborers who were kept near mines and factories but away from white residential areas. The students and peers filed off the bus and began looking around and talking with locals. But one of our white students refused to get off the bus, proclaiming, "You're not keeping us safe!" as she sobbed with her head on her seat. Some of the peer educators expressed sympathy and tried to reassure her. Others were simply puzzled by the way she read signs of poverty as indications of danger. One black male peer said that he felt personally offended, because she was essentially refusing to acknowledge his daily life, while ignoring his reassurance and refusing to acknowledge how her own privilege shaped her perceptions. Mieke expresses both her anger and her empathy, highlighting the opportunity for reflection that the incident provided.

> I mean the hostels are historically so important in South Africa, and . . . the uprisings that happened . . . And I

think that's part of my frustration with her as well, is I kind of wanted to say, not only are you not taking notice of what you might be saying to the peer educators, but also . . . don't you understand how monumental being allowed into this setting is? And that, I, I actually had to spend the rest of the afternoon kind of like making sure that I stayed away from her. . . . It just brought up a whole lot of emotions that I think I knew at the time were probably unfair . . . if you're 18 or 19 from a relatively sheltered background, that it is completely overwhelming, and then to a certain extent you are allowed to respond to that. I just kind of wanted to shake her and say like, "How dare you! This is the reality, not just of the people living here, but also some of the peer educators!" . . . the impact that it had on the peer educators. But at the same time that's not something that you can . . . can't prevent that. And it's probably good for everybody involved to have that experience. (Mieke, white peer educator)

Insights into the Effectiveness and Limitations of the Peer Education Model

Although the peer educators developed an astute set of critiques about the students' foibles, they nonetheless characterized them as eager participants in the peer education model. While the peers were aware of the various academic assignments the students had to complete—often with the peers' assistance—these were rarely mentioned in the interviews. The effectiveness of the course, in their view, resulted from the abundant time that peers and students spent together, and the rapport that flourished as a result. Dialogue on race is also cited repeatedly to illustrate the potency of interactions with the students.

The peers frequently connect structured activities to students asking questions, emphasizing that the real learning occurs in the interaction between peer and student. Nhlanhla references a visit to the Apartheid Museum, which prompted many students to ask about the success of the post-Apartheid era.

> "Oh, like we went to the Apartheid Museum and I mean, things were quite bad. But is it still so bad now?" You know, and, having to tell them our experiences. . . . Like I just feel like that was just so much more enlightening. (Nhlanhla, black peer educator).

Nhlanhla makes a similar comment about the many lectures that the peers and students attended together. In this instance, she asserts that her experience of segregation at her university is more salient than the lectures they attended.

> I go to Wits [University] . . . like I don't know how to explain this, but like in terms of segregation on campus? You know, it wasn't something we discussed in the lectures, but having like one of the students come up to me to ask me about that, it was so much more easier for me to sort of like explain to them that, you know, these kinds of things still do happen, even though it's not as bad as it used to be. . . . And it was so much easier for them to see . . . from my perspective than it was from a lecture. And even though we were in the lecture and everybody concentrates and like took notes. (Nhlanhla)

Nhlanhla illustrates the opportunity to learn from the lived experience of the peers in reference to her own township upbringing.

> But like . . . I feel like being with me and actually just sharing my experiences they actually, they learned a lot about what it, I mean, I was a young black girl from Soweto. And I don't know, I feel like they just got to see a very

> different side from everything that they sort of like know
> about people from the township or how we're supposed
> to be like. . . . I just feel like they learned a lot about South
> African experience. They learned a lot about, about what
> it was like us growing up in the township. (Nhlanhla)

Mieke credits the students with choosing to engage beyond the minimum requirements of the course, enabling them to benefit from the "space for dialogue."

> You know, they did the reading, they did your assign-
> ments, and, you know, we are fun to hang out with, and
> you know, that's where it ends. But, my overwhelming
> sense of that, that time that I spent with your students
> was there was so much space for dialogue, and . . . that
> even if there was just one of them who asked a question,
> like, at the end of the conversation there'd be six or seven
> people involved in it. And I think that people like talking
> about themselves. So, it does work well from that per-
> spective because if the students are prepared to ask the
> questions, the peer educators will happily talk. (Mieke)

The dialogue was heavily dependent on the unstructured time that was woven into the busy schedule kept by the students and peers. As Comfort points out, even the long stretches on the bus provided meaningful learning opportunities.

> You know, you brought those students and then you also
> managed to get some South African students, and you
> know. Just getting them together, and let them flow and
> whatever happens, happens. That's what I was seeing. I
> mean where we were sitting in the bus, you know, no-
> tice that peer educators were . . . just sitting randomly in
> around the bus with all the students, just mingling and

> . . . I mean even for me, most of the learning actually took place . . . hanging out and chilling and doing all these things. (Comfort, Black peer educator)

Diversity within the peer educator group is cited frequently as a resource for teaching the students about the heterogeneity of South African culture and racial identity, and for opening up dialogue about race. Asanda highlights the opportunity to learn about differences among peers of different races, but also within racial groups.

> You could chat to Rob and feel like, "I can relate a bit more to Rob," and chat to me like, and be like, "She's completely different!" . . . So you're not getting a sense of South African culture, but different cultures within South Africa. . . . But also there's an expectation that just because you are black and you are black, you should sort of understand each other. . . . Okay, I think actually did come up, because I had one of the students come up to me, he's like, "You're black and so-and-so is also black. But you're completely different. How come?" (Asanda, black peer educator)

According to Charles, dialogue on race did not come easily, but emerged as rapport expanded between the two groups.

> I would say they've learned a lot, basically because most of your students were white, right? And yeah, and we're black. And initially, there was this kind of resistance between us, but as they got used to us and we actually talked about the racial issue . . . So it actually opened their eyes. . . . And we talked more about it, even the discussions, even though we were just chilling around and yeah. It made them to be aware that racism is around and how . . . to actually confront those particular situations. And

> they even told the same thing that even in the USA, it is
> still happening. So, we kind of like on the same page and
> understood each other. (Charles, black peer educator)

Reflections on the Value of the Program
for the Peer Educators

We were initially inattentive to the potential value of the course for the peers beyond their salary and curiosity about meeting a group of young Americans. As the peers began to help us understand the travel course as a two-way street, we saw that both groups valued many of the same things, not least personal connections with their age-mates. As the peers and students conducted joint participant-observation, the peers welcomed the chance to learn more about American culture, and to unlearn the many stereotypes they carried about Americans. Yet learning about South Africa and befriending South Africans of other races was in many cases a significant experience. In addition, spaces for dialogue about race and racism is a theme woven through many of the interviews. All these cases help demonstrate the profound impact that direct experience of "the Other" can have on understanding across perceived divides of identity (as Adams and Damron demonstrate in the case of community integration of people with Autism Spectrum Disorder, this volume).

Despite the short period in the field, the quality of the time allowed for the start of many meaningful friendships. Ori notes that these took place between the two groups, but also among the peers.

> That you really did come out with friends, you did come
> out with relationships. That even though we were togeth-
> er for a very short period of time. Even within that short
> period of time . . . it's . . . I really felt I could turn to a
> lot of the American students and to peer educators who

> I hadn't met before. And really treat them as very close friends. (Ori, white peer educator)

Noma describes her emotions at the end of the course, and also how the sense of connection helped the group overcome disagreements.

> I learned a lot and I cannot overemphasize that enough. And it was also an emotional experience. . . . And I really felt I connected with some of the students. . . . I was surprised. . . . I was actually crying at the airport and I couldn't believe I had that experience in such a short period of time that I connected. I was amazed with that myself, where we grew to know each other. We disagreed hectically. . . . But at the same time, you come back together again, and you pick up each other's conversations and you iron things out if there was any offense or anything like that. (Noma)

While the emphasis in the course was on the American students learning from the peers as a complement to the course content, peers described learning new things directly from the students as well. Asanda talks about interacting with one of the American students who was a lesbian, and the experience of having her own ideas challenged.

> I think, I think interacting with people who've got a completely different background from yours, it challenges some of your views about things . . . one of the people in the group was a lesbian, and I didn't know. And I had my certain views about it. And it so happened that the person was doing research on views about lesbians and gays in South Africa. And she had me make a comment . . . [but] she didn't tell me she was lesbian. . . . And she

> was just talking, and we're talking, and I was telling her
> how I feel. And, her questions kept challenging . . . So
> how come you think this way about this? And after she
> left, I thought about some of [these] things. (Asanda)

The peers valued learning about the United States from an "insider perspective," and welcomed the chance to be disabused of stereotypes, positive or negative. Charles describes realizing he idealized the United States a little too much.

> So long as you are living in America, therefore you have
> a brighter future. But that was not the case. They told me
> that there were a lot of like drug cases . . . maybe when it's
> high school. . . . I thought that this was the problem we
> were facing in South Africa or Africa in general. But they
> told me that they are actually experiencing that particu-
> lar thing. (Charles)

In addition to obtaining new information, some stereotypes were dispelled through observation. Asanda and Comfort make similar comments about unlearning stereotypes through direct experience of the students.

> I was very anti-American. . . . But interacting with them
> . . . it helped me also correct my misconceptions about
> Americans because I just grouped all of them into that
> crowd. And I don't like them. But then you get to see . . .
> even if they are Americans, they are people. (Asanda)

> So it doesn't necessarily make me to sit down and one
> day I asked them questions and then they said, "No! We
> don't do that in the U.S." or "No, we're not like that." It
> was just through observing and just being with them
> that I was able to have some of the stereotypes actually
> be erased. (Comfort)

The opportunity to see new sights and sounds through the course enabled the peers to learn new things about South African society. Ori mentions a trip to Katlehong Township where he would ordinarily not go.

> Going to Katlehong, going to places, really also gave me a sense of, you know, wow! There is so much in this country that I'm overlooking. You know, and so much that I still have to explore. (Ori)

Asanda and Charles both describe the shock of seeing examples of South African poverty close-up.

> Especially with the visits to Soweto, to those places where you really see poverty, it, I think it opened up not just their eyes but our eyes. Because some things were a shocker for me too. (Asanda)

> Basically, I was suddenly travelling. I was kind of like embarrassed. Knowing people from outside expect you to know better about your culture . . . And I was not like that, I was like them, I was shocked as they were. And that particular thing made me to, to want to research more, and I did the research. (Charles)

For Noma, making new discoveries about South Africa activated her sense of patriotism.

> I mean, if I had to sum it all up, I would say it had made me patriotic. You know, where I was surprised with the amazement with certain things and made me appreciate the country more. (Noma)

Several of the peers described social taboos surrounding talking about race. Mieke notes an attitude that downplays the importance of dialogue about race.

> There's no dialogue happening in South Africa at the
> moment. . . . The overwhelming sense that you get is like,
> get on with it. You know, it's just sort like don't talk about
> it just do it. (Mieke)

In some instances, the course appears to have given the South
African peers more room to discuss race vis-à-vis the students.
Mieke describes how she sees group interaction among students and
peers creating a new "safe space," suggesting that the presence of the
Americans helped to displace some of the tensions that ordinarily
suppress discussion.

> This sort of almost triangle of interactions of the black
> South African peers, the white South African peers, and
> the American students and how it, how the groups in-
> teracted . . . there's a strange dynamic of creating a safe
> space because although the South Africans were not
> that comfortable talking about the issues because there's
> the outsider, the outsiders are there. Suddenly, it's a safe
> space and you're happy to say things that you, you know,
> wouldn't necessarily talk about. (Mieke)

Dialogue about race in the context of South Africa's brutal history of racism is difficult to schedule. The strength of our model
may lie in the fact that it is adaptive enough to stay out of the way
and allow people to talk on their own terms. At one fortuitous
dinner that included peers, students, and an array of South African
colleagues and friends of different races, a large-group discussion
began spontaneously, thanks to the generosity of the participants.
A white university professor who had been active in the struggle
against Apartheid talked about how alienated he now felt in a less
"European" South Africa. One of the black peer educators talked

about how far away Apartheid seemed to him personally, but how proud he felt of his older relatives who had been courageous in the resistance movement. Mieke's mother was also present, and Mieke heard her talk for the first time about being a member of the *Black Sash* movement—a group made up of white women who joined the struggle against Apartheid. In her interview, Mieke recalls her experience of the evening and what it was like to listen to her mother.

> That evening that we had dinner . . . where people had an opportunity to speak about their experiences . . . there was also, once that was over, there was just kind of mingling and hanging out and being able to go and follow-up on you know, "You said this, I found that really interesting." I thought that that evening was definitely something worth trying to, to recreate if possible . . . I mean, that was an amazing evening for me as well. Now I actually, because my mom spoke. And you know, we, there are very few opportunities where as a child you get to hear your parents speak in that kind of context. (Mieke)

Listening to the Peer Educators: Improvements to the Course

Recognizing the impact that a travel course with American students can have on peer educators, we now view the course as a reciprocal experience that needs to be planned with the needs of both groups of young people in mind. The peers' critiques and suggestions have proved helpful in this regard, and will shape future travel courses. These are the changes we hope to make:

1. Spend the first week of January-term in Johannesburg rather than on campus. This would add significantly to the cost of the course but would carry several benefits. We could introduce the

peers and students earlier in the process, and provide classroom-based preparation for both groups. The course could have a stronger comparative element, e.g., reviewing the history of race in both countries side-by-side.

2. Provide training for the peer educators with South African experts on inter-group facilitation. This would allow for more explicit focus on dialogues on race. It would also give both groups a skill set in facilitated dialogues that they can use beyond the bounds of the course.

3. Provide certification for the peer educators. After working very hard for three weeks, the peers made it clear that they had learned a lot but had no credential to show for it that might be useful for future employment or educational opportunities. Developing certificates in consultation with South African university authorities would enable us to fill this need.

Conclusion

Short-term international travel courses can achieve a range of worthwhile goals, from "tourism with books" to high quality cultural immersion in which locals and visitors feel respected and enriched. As we began to plan this course, our aspiration to reach for the latter felt tenuous. We bemoaned our own poor preparation to help students get more out of a visit to the Apartheid Museum than the fleeting sensations of horror and hope any American might feel passing through on vacation. Finding culturally appropriate, abundant, and safe ways for our students to engage in ethnographic activities seemed like a crapshoot, and certainly not something we could build a three-week course around. The value of a course in which we would provide a deep sense of the culture while also teaching field methods preoccupied us, yet felt elusive. Once the idea of South African peer educators dawned on us, we became more hopeful.

Now our imagined American students leaving a lecture from a South African scholar would have a South African undergraduate pondering the meaning—or griping about the tedium—at their side. Now there was a chance for real rapport to have a chance to build, making "in-depth ethnographic interviewing" worth teaching (for us) and worth attempting (for the students).

During the first days of the course we could see that amid the budding friendships and nearly endless conversations, key issues such as race were not following a simple pattern of "South Africans teach Americans about the enduring legacy of Apartheid." Instead, black and white South Africans and black and white Americans were engaging in complex discussions that involved a fair measure of conflict and frustration as well as insight and new understanding. Our perspective on the nature of the course began to shift when we first heard a black South African peer tell us this was the first time he had spoken with a white South African, and so we turned our attention more to the peers' experiences. As we began to listen to the peers elaborate on their own participant-observation with the Americans, we realized that it was inadequate to conceptualize the fieldwork experience as unidirectional. As we contemplated conducting research on the course, our interest expanded from pedagogical effectiveness for the students to questions about the benefits for the peers: What were they learning from the Americans about the United States? What skill sets were they developing that could be valuable beyond the bounds of the course? How was their own understanding of race and racism being challenged and expanded in unique ways through this experience? What features of a peer education model—such as international dialogue groups on race—could be applied in other contexts, perhaps with more wide-ranging results?

Lastly, we do not want to overstate the case for our insights into how anthropologists grapple with received notions about where "the field" is located and how ethnographic encounters ought to be structured. This is, after all, a three-week travel course. We have sought primarily to assess and recommend a pedagogical method for undergraduate international education. At the same time, viewing the peer education model in action has given us a chance to reflect on how the nature of ethnography changes when we start with the blending of members of two cultural groups, in contrast with more conventional approaches. Similarly, questions about *where* ethnography takes place may shift when cultural informants carve out their own distinct terrain separate (symbolically, and perhaps even geographically) from the dominant surroundings. Thus the "local" focus of anthropology may sometimes be less a function of where anthropologists travel to than of the spaces they create after they arrive.

WORKS CITED

Clifford, James. 1988. *The Predicament of Culture: Twentieth Century Ethnography, Literature, and Art.* Cambridge, MA: Harvard University Press.

Crabtree, Robbin. 2013. "The Intended and Unintended Consequences of International Service Learning." *Journal of Higher Education Outreach and Engagement* 17 (2): 43–65.

Goldstein, Daniel M. 2012. *Outlawed: Between Security and Rights in a Bolivian City.* Durham, NC: Duke University Press.

Gupta, Akhil, and James Ferguson, eds. 1997. *Anthropological Locations: Boundaries and Grounds of a Field Science.* Berkeley: University of California Press.

Hannerz, Ulf. 2003. "Being there . . . and there . . . and there! Reflections on Multi-Site Ethnography." *Ethnography* 4 (2): 201–216.

Klaaren, Kristen J, Scott London, and Jonathan E. Klaaren. 2006. "Peering Into the Future: Internationalizing Education with Experiential Peer Learning." In *The Internationalization of Higher Education in South Africa*, edited by Roshen Kishun, 145–151. Durban, South Africa: International Education Association of South Africa.

Lassiter, Luke E. 2001. "From 'Reading over the Shoulders of Natives" to "Reading Alongside Natives,' Literally: Toward a Collaborative and Reciprocal Ethnography." *Journal of Anthropological Research* 57 (2): 137–149.

Low, Setha M., and Sally Engle Merry. 2010. "Engaged Anthropology: Diversity and Dilemmas." *Current Anthropology* 51 (S2): S203–S226.

Marcus, George E and Michael M.J. Fischer. 1986. *Anthropology as Cultural Critique: An Experimental Moment in the Human Sciences.* Chicago: University of Chicago Press.

Modan, Gabriella. 2016. "Writing the Relationship: Ethnographer-Informant Interactions in the New Media Era." *Journal of Linguistic Anthropology* 26 (1): 98–107.

Nickols, Sharon Y., Nancy J. Rothenberg, Lioba Moshi, and Meredith Tetloff. 2013. "International Service-Learning: Students' Personal Challenges and Intercultural Competence." *Journal of Higher Education Outreach and Engagement* 17 (4): 97–124.

Rabinow, Paul. 1977. *Reflections on Fieldwork in Morocco.* Berkeley: University of California Press.

Rosaldo, Renato. 1989. *Culture and Truth: The Remaking of Social Analysis.* Boston: Beacon Press.

Becoming an Ally:
How Communities Can Empower and Embrace Individuals with Autism Spectrum Disorder

Hillary Adams and Eugenia Damron

Introduction

There is a demographic shift going on in the United States. The Centers for Disease Control (2015) estimates that one in sixty-eight children are diagnosed with Autism Spectrum Disorder (ASD). In just ten years, the prevalence has increased from one in 150—a huge leap from the 1960s and '70s when the diagnosis was approximately one in two thousand (Centers for Disease Control 2015). As the number of individuals with ASD rises, average citizens must realize the responsibility to embrace this growing population and better engage in personal efforts to assist individuals with autism to integrate effectively into their communities. Individuals with autism are isolated, often trapped by their own self-doubt, challenges with communication, and trepidations of fitting a societal mold. Average citizens have the keys to open these doors by opening their minds to those who are different. People with ASD need allies to support them to connect, exchange, and make a positive impact within the community.

Autism Spectrum Disorder is identified through two main indicators. The American Psychiatric Association, through the Diagnostic and Statistical Manual 5 (2013), lists the first indicator as persistent deficits in social communication and interaction; these deficits can manifest through atypical social-emotional reciprocity, lack of nonverbal communicative behaviors, and deficits in developing, maintaining, and understanding relationships (27-28). The second indicator of ASD is restricted, repetitive patterns of behavior, interests, or activities (28). These symptoms play out through repetitive motor movements, use of objects, or speech; insistence on sameness, routines, or patterns of verbal or nonverbal behavior; restricted, fixated interests that are abnormal in intensity; and hyper- or hypo-reactivity to sensory input (28). Autism Spectrum Disorder can range in severity, from Level 1 (requiring minimal support) to Level 3 (requiring very substantial support). No matter the severity, adults diagnosed with ASD often yearn to lead meaningful lives on their own terms. A quality life involves varying levels of independence, postsecondary education, employment (Hansen 2015), socialization, and romantic or sexual relationships (Hellemans et al. 2006, 94).

An average of fifty thousand individuals with ASD will turn eighteen each year in the United States; however, adult services continue to be sparse (Roux et al. 2013, 931). As many families plan to celebrate high school graduations as a joyous event, families of graduates diagnosed with ASD will face the daunting question, "What's next?" Families must face the edge of a cliff, wondering what services their state can provide, whether their family will qualify for these services, as well as if college or independent living are options for their sons and daughters. Across the United States, adult services are available, but limited. In West Virginia, there are several initiatives in place to serve adults with ASD: the West Virginia Developmental Disabilities Council assists with training and grants to enhance community partnership; the WV Division of Rehabilitation Services helps individuals with ASD reach vocational goals; and the WV Autism Training Center provides a variety of Positive Behavior

Support direct services and has established the Marshall University College Program for Students with Autism Spectrum Disorder. In addition, Title XIX Home and Community Based waivers can assist with service payment for low-income families, providing things like private nursing, care management, and medical equipment for those who are limited in functioning. Wait lists, family income, provider criteria, or lack of funding, however, can inhibit involvement or depth of services provided. Given the current inadequate number of services, everyone has a powerful obligation to create change: We can embrace individuals with ASD by developing citizen understanding and skill sets related to the diagnosis. Change can happen by a conversation at the dinner table, advocating in a workplace, or a simple hello. We empower those around us to accept individuals with autism if we challenge ourselves to connect.

Evolution of Autism Services

The twentieth century progressed from institutionalizing and sterilizing individuals with ASD to emphasizing concepts of self-determination and inclusion. Service providers stopped labeling the population "unworthy of life" and now, instead, discuss "quality of life." For our communities to continue to make positive steps in advocacy, we must also recognize how far we have come. Beginning in the 1920s, the United States saw the legalization of sterilization in seventeen states and the rise of eugenics, while the 1930s and 1940s encouraged the institutionalization of children deemed "defective" (Donvan and Zucker 2016). In the 1950s and 1960s, when autism was believed to be a personality disorder, the serotonin-inhibiting drug, LSD, was a focus of experiments. Additionally, the "refrigerator mother" theory, depicting a lack of maternal warmth shown to a child, also became a popular theory for the development of autism (Baker 2013, 1090). In the 1970s, electric shock therapy was practiced on children with autism as a type of aversive punishment. The late 1970s and early 1980s saw massive deinstitutionalizations, and mental health treatment shifted from hospitals to the community. Neuroscience had an increasingly important role in mental health in the 1990s and 2000s, while autism awareness and research increased dramatically. Today, Applied Behavior Analysis (introduced in the 1960s) and Positive Behavior Support (introduced in the 1980s) are two of the most widely used therapies for Autism Spectrum Disorder. Both Applied Behavior Analysis and Positive Behavior Support focus on the science of Behavior Learning Theory—reducing undesired behavior and reinforcing the positive ones. Many believe the difference in the two interventions relies on Positive Behavior Support's emphasis on quality of life, normalization, and choice (Weiss et al. 2009, 428).

Before this evolution of thinking, Leo Kanner of Johns Hopkins University sought to understand the unique behavior of a patient who was displaying what is now called Autism Spectrum Disorder. In 1942, Kanner used the phrase, "autistic disturbances of affective contact," pulling from a portion of the schizophrenia diagnosis, to describe his patients' inability to relate themselves to other people. Kanner was calling for the humanization of the mentally feeble, while others were calling for mercy killings (Donvan and Zucker 2016). In the 1950s and 1960s, autism was identified as a form of childhood schizophrenia. Kanner made important strides in his career to distinguish autism from schizophrenia, as well as from mental retardation. In 1980, his efforts were realized in the DSM-III, when autism was listed as a pervasive developmental disorder with three basic criteria, which was then expanded upon in 1987 with the DSM-III-R listing eight to sixteen criteria (Baker 2013, 1091).

A significant cultural shift originally began in the 1970s with the advent of the self-advocacy movement, giving voices to the previously stifled. This movement really took shape in the 1990s and 2000s, as the use of the Internet became more prevalent, tying autism communities together. For the first time, individuals with autism, and their families, were able to unite with one another in a broader sense to create connections. These communities, as described by Holland et al. (1998), are "figured worlds," giving meaning to people's interaction and changing historically due to political or social values of the community. Figured worlds are socially organized encounters in which an individual's position matters (45). This discourse amongst the autism community provided a contrast to the biomedical definition, and, instead, focused on neurodiversity (Bagatell 2010, 38). Finally, individuals with ASD were not lesser humans to be cured or isolated, but people with differences worthy of support and understanding.

Integrating individuals with ASD into our communities through education is vital so that we can reach into the culture and world in which they live. To take an ethnographic view, we first need to understand the complexity of mapping the diverse world of autism. Imagine you are from a non-English speaking country and you arrive in the United States to study American culture. You decide that New York City is a good place to begin. Upon arrival, you realize the cultures within the Bronx, Manhattan, Brooklyn, Queens, and Staten Island are vastly different. Not only that, but your translator can only vaguely communicate and interpret the events in which you are submerged. To simplify the experiences of individuals with ASD as the same would be like depicting the same cultural experiences of Manhattan and the Bronx. Additionally, due to typical barriers in communication, asking an individual with ASD to depict their world experience may be like relying on poor translation in a foreign land. This is why we must educate each other to recognize commonalities within the diagnosis first and welcome opportunities for deeper understanding of the human experience of individuals with ASD as a result. By creating a conceptual framework of autism through training and education, forming meaningful, working relationships with individuals with ASD becomes less intimidating. We must build a community that is open to change, and immerse ourselves in a world where difference is not scary—it is just different.

Ally Recruitment: Removing the Double-Edged Sword

Communities have the ability to reshape societal standards for a more inclusive and compassionate environment for those with ASD. Howlin (2000) expresses that for individuals with ASD, there is "constant pressure to 'fit in' with the demands of a society that fails to understand their needs or difficulties. Inability to meet these demands may lead to stress and anxiety and even psychiatric breakdown" (79).

Within the United States, our prevailing culture screams, "dance to the beat of your own drum," "different is beautiful," and "don't be afraid to be yourself!" Then, society leans in to whisper, "don't dance too loudly, don't be too different, and only be yourself if we approve." Our culture cherishes uniqueness in theory, but we hand out puzzle pieces to individuals with ASD, reminding them they do not quite fit the mold of society. As citizens, however, we must meet them somewhere in the middle, not only to support quality lives for this growing population, but so we can grow as individuals, as communities, and as a society.

Our nation, like many others, has nurtured an ableist society—the notion that people are automatically better, have better lives, or have better brains or bodies because they are not disabled. Even more defeating, is how those with disabilities internalize ableism. Individuals with ASD learn they are tolerated in society, rather than accepted.

By gaining understanding and then including individuals with ASD, we can tap into a completely underutilized resource. The following personal narrative illustrates this point:

I recently helped a young man, diagnosed with autism, to fill out an application for a railroad switch operator. He is a recent graduate with an affinity for all things railroad and would be an ideal candidate. He can stay up for long hours, does not mind tedious or seemingly mundane tasks, and would absorb his roles efficiently and enthusiastically. As we neared the end of the application, however, we faced the inevitable double-edged sword: to disclose or not to disclose. Most individuals with ASD, and with the capacity to work, will face this dilemma. By not disclosing, he could face an interviewer who would not understand his pauses in speech, his interrupted eye contact, or his lack of work history. To disclose means he could face stigma and discrimination, never receiving the invitation for an interview. As a young adult well versed in ableism, he clung to not disclosing. After weighing the pros and cons, however, he gambled on disclosure, hoping his true self would be enough.

Passing on disclosing, as described by Leary (1999), cited in Campbell (2007, 10), "represents a form of self-protection that nevertheless usually disables, and sometimes destroys, the self it means to safeguard." Individuals with disabilities should not have to mask themselves to feel included. By resisting the ableist mentality and adopting the ally mentality, we can provide an environment where individuals with ASD can openly discuss their diagnosis without hesitation and without fear of backlash.

The resistance against an ableist society, additionally, comes with its own double-edged sword. Because our society is so resistant to discussing limitations as a result of a disability, we extinguish honest conversations. We believe that to identify and openly discuss how a disability affects someone's everyday life is to diminish him or her as a human. This is not so.

WV Autism Training Center

As allies, we want to have that honest conversation—to connect with each other as members of communities with shared interests. The West Virginia Autism Training Center, located at Marshall University, created the "Allies Supporting Autism Spectrum Diversity" training to help with common misconceptions regarding individuals with ASD. Checking out in a grocery store, applying for a job, or eating at a restaurant can be a daunting task for an individual with ASD. But it does not have to be. What if the grocery cashier understood that not being able to purchase a brand of cereal could throw off desired routines? What if the job interviewer recognized that speech delays are due to slow processing speed, not low IQ? What if the restaurant server showed empathy to the patron overstimulated by clanging dishes and loud chatter? The Allies Supporting Autism Spectrum Diversity training works to inform and educate individuals who wish to provide a safe and accepting environment for individuals living with Autism Spectrum Disorder. Our mission is to advocate for diversity and promote understanding in order to support and develop ASD awareness.

The ally mentality is being quickly embedded into Marshall University, and we are spreading our ideals through our Huntington, West Virginia, home. Winner of the national competition and named "America's Best Community," Huntington, West Virginia, stands as an example that change is not only possible, but also wanted by our citizens. As our city works to revitalize and beautify its outward appearance through the Huntington Innovation Project, we seek to revitalize and beautify our city from the inside. Through the understanding, acceptance, and inclusion of a misunderstood and underutilized population, we can help to nurture productive members of society. Individuals with ASD wish for independence, employment, friendships, and community inclusion. It is our job to meet them halfway by learning what we can do to support those goals. We need citizen involvement to create change—to shift responsibility from mental health experts to citizens who wish to spread autism advocacy into our communities. Our hope is to chisel away at the rock and hard place individuals with ASD are stuck between. They should be able to openly discuss the need for support, disclose without fear, and grow up understanding they are capable of living meaningful lives absent of ableist attitudes.

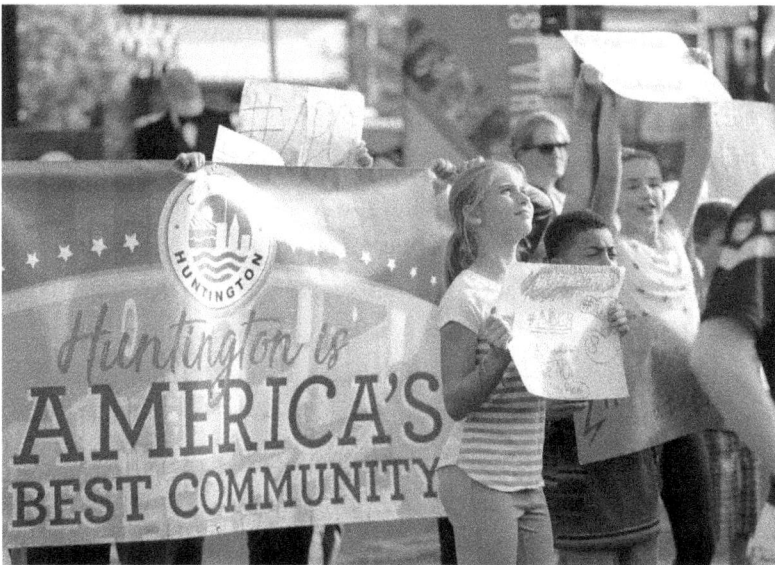

"America's Best Community" competiton
(Photo by Lori Wolfe, *The Herald-Dispatch*, Huntington, West Virginia)

Societal Stigma

Due to misconceptions caused by a lack of understanding of Autism Spectrum Disorder, there is often stigma associated with the diagnosis. This obloquy follows myths and stereotypes that are inaccurate and often unkind. ASD stigma can inhibit educational opportunities, employment, socialization, and independent living. Awareness is growing, but stigma continues to exist, and individuals with ASD are affected in a variety of ways. Some individuals avoid disclosing their diagnosis for fear of being placed in a box, leading to different or unfair treatment. Others diagnosed with ASD may absorb that stigma, creating self-doubt and untapped potential. Because they are misunderstood, individuals with ASD are avoided, leading to reduced learning opportunities in socialization and communication, as well as loneliness. As humans, we resist actions that may lead to discomfort or uncertainty, but relish in moments when we take those risks. These tiny "risks" for communities, however, could lead to life-altering impacts for individuals with autism.

In a research study by Jacoby (2015), seventy-seven community members were surveyed regarding "comfortability" with individuals with ASD. Responses on a zero to ten scale, zero being extremely uncomfortable and ten being extremely comfortable, had varying results dependent on social situation. Jacoby (2015) explains that the more ongoing contact with someone with ASD, the more likely an individual was to feel comfortable with interactions (30). Participants showed the lowest comfort levels in professional settings (cashier, coworker, waiter, or doctor) with average comfortability being 6.60—the very lowest being if the individual with ASD were their doctor, with an average 4.82 comfortability. When searching as to whether the type of previous experience with individuals with ASD effects comfort levels, two experiences showed positive correlations: "I have learned about autism at school or work" had a .27

positive correlation, while "I have had a job related to working with people with autism" had a .28 correlation with higher comfortability (Jacoby 2015, 26). It is clear the more exposure and one-on-one interactions community members allow themselves to engage in, the higher comfort they will feel in future exchanges with individuals with ASD.

Previous research regarding efforts to reduce autism stigma within the elementary education setting provides further evidence that exposure to people with autism can lead to less stigma. Campbell (2006) sought to encourage persuasive communication through autism disclosure of children in order to create attitude and behavioral change in the classroom. Research suggests that by initially introducing ASD to classrooms, we can create inclusive education and positive initial attitudes of peer responses toward individuals with ASD (Campbell 2006, 268-269), which could potentially lead to a more knowledgeable and accepting society.

In a 2010 study at the University of Hong Kong by Ling, Mak, and Cheng, an examination of attitudes of "frontline workers" (123 teachers and faculty who worked directly with students with ASD to age eighteen) was conducted to empirically investigate the stigma of students with autism. Results showed that better knowledge and longer working experience with autism correlated with low intentions to punish the student. Those who previously received special education training were more confident in how to handle situations with students with ASD, therefore indicating training was important to frontline staff. Although training was linked to better preparedness, stigma toward ASD was still apparent. The role of emotions, like anger and sympathy, appears to have a direct influence on the behavioral intentions toward students with autism, suggesting training on emotion regulation and alternative teaching methods could be useful.

Staniland and Byrne (2013) aimed to bridge the gaps in ASD anti-stigma literature by evaluating the effects of an anti-stigma program on adolescent boys regarding their peers with ASD. The study involved a multi-session intervention with direct contact and videos displaying individuals with ASD. Results indicated that knowledge and attitude had a positive correlation with the training, but not behavioral intentions to engage with peers.

Gillespie-Lynch et al. (2015) conducted a brief online training with college students in order to increase knowledge and decrease stigma. Similar to Staniland and Byrne's outcomes, immediate increases in knowledge were shown. However, changes in knowledge were relatively greater than changes in stigma, suggesting stigma is more difficult to alter. Common misconceptions of typical college students found in this study state that ASD is associated with the following: cognitive difficulties or lack of intelligence, vaccinations, the inability to engage in romantic relationships, and the likelihood of pursuing STEM subjects. This research saw marginal improvement of these stigmas post-training (Gillespie-Lynch et al. 2015).

Although trainings and up-to-date knowledge regarding ASD are shown to improve understanding, a theme has emerged from this research that although positive change is often seen in mindsets, behaviors and actions toward individuals with ASD are less susceptible to change. Our understanding and initiatives to reduce stigma and cultivate more inclusive communities must continue to develop.

Postsecondary Education

Higher education is a daunting prospect for individuals with autism and their families; it is particularly scary for those looking to move away from home. Individuals with ASD often need very tailored and structured support, therefore making it difficult for traditional disability service programs within higher education to meet the true needs of students with ASD. Of the 190 to 192 higher education institutions surveyed, based off the *Benchmarks of Effective Supports for College Students with Asperger's Disorder,* 12.5 percent have fully dedicated staff who assist instructors in improving academic outcomes for students with ASD, while only 7.3 percent have staff dedicated to working directly with the students (Ellison 2013, 61). These support programs vary significantly in format, practices, and prices, but provide hope to many students and their families in pursuing the dream of a college degree. The higher education community is seeing a significant increase in the admission of individuals with ASD, which comes with a unique set of challenges; collaborative practices that foster growth are pertinent to the development of best practices to serve these students with ASD (Ackles, Fields, and Skinner 2013).

Based on the National Center for Educational Statistics' nationally representative sample of two- and four-year colleges and universities, data indicated that 2 percent of students registered with a disability reported having ASD, and 56 percent of colleges and universities reported at least one enrolled student with ASD (Raue and Lewis 2011, 18). This likely underestimates the true numbers of individuals with ASD enrolled in higher education (Matthews, Ly, and Goldberg 2014) due to lack of diagnosis or lack of disclosure. Shattuck et al. (2012) found the rate of postsecondary education among those with ASD, particularly within the first two years after high school, was lower than for those with a speech/language impairment or learning disability, but higher than those with mental retardation (1046).

As students with ASD enter college campuses in higher numbers, the need for more comprehensive services grows. Students, by disclosing their diagnosis, can receive accommodations through their disability office; typical auxiliary services include extended time on exams, notetaking, taped text, and private testing space (US Equal

Employment Opportunity Commission). These accommodations, however, are not often the comprehensive support that these students need. Cai and Richdale's research (2016) noted that "of the twenty-two students attending higher education with ASD that were interviewed, most students (63.6%) felt their educations needs were satisfied, however their social needs were not met. Fifteen students lost interest in university activities or coursework; ten of these students mentioned wishing they had someone to motivate them" (34). Additionally, students who may have difficulty in academics or socialization in higher education often do not seek assistance, possibly because they are concerned with stigmas attached to their diagnosis. A participant in the Cai and Richdale (2016) focus group noted that he or she had no help and "didn't want to be treated differently, I didn't want to be treated like I had some kind of disease, which I think sometimes we are treated like, like we're lesser people" (35). This type of internalized ableist thinking is common among individuals with ASD. Research shows, however, that knowledge of a diagnosis may actually improve attitudes toward college students with ASD.

Matthews, Ly, and Goldberg (2014) conducted a study of 224 college students' perceptions of vignettes depicting ASD behaviors with either the label of "High Functioning Autism," "typical college student," or "no label." They found that students reported a more positive disposition toward hypothetical peers given the label of High Functioning Autism as compared to those having no label (96). It is possible that with more disclosure and campus community awareness, individuals with ASD will experience more inclusion. It is important for policy-makers and administrators to be aware of the positive attitudes of college students towards the inclusion of individuals with intellectual disabilities in order to encourage the expansion of inclusive programs in colleges and universities (Griffin et al. 2012).

With a more accepting and understanding higher education community, students may feel inclined to be open about their diagnosis, leading them to the supports, accommodations, and personnel that can help them succeed. Persistent concern of stigma and isolation due to a diagnosis means students will continue to enter campuses without disclosing, often becoming a number in a university retention rate. Research on retention notes that feelings of belongingness achieved through involvement in activities inside and outside the classroom are integral to learning, and ultimately to the students' success (Matthews, Ly, and Goldberg 2014). Marshall University, year after year, strives to create a community where students with autism belong, feel included, and have a network of allies. It is important for this dedication to students with ASD to spread throughout the higher education communities of the United States, and infiltrate the towns they call home.

Employment

Post high school and college employment for individuals with disabilities continues to be one of the most pressing concerns for adults with Autism Spectrum Disorder. It is clear that the majority of individuals with disabilities do not attain a satisfactory level of career development consistent with their capabilities (Brolin and Gysbers 1989). Developing students to their maximum ability is one of the foundations of education in order to prepare for employment, develop social skills, and function independently (Brolin and Gysbers 1989); however, addressing unemployment continues to be a struggle.

One of the most powerful ways community members can effectively create meaningful change is through providing employment opportunities for individuals with autism. By simply gaining basic knowledge of the diagnosis through training, community members are more likely to recognize that behaviors linked to ASD do not discredit the ability to do a job well. According to The Autism Society of America (2015), in 2014, only 19.3 percent of people with disabilities in the United States were participating in the labor force (working or seeking work). Of those, 12.9 percent were unemployed, leaving only 16.8 percent of the population with disabilities employed, compared to 69.3 percent of those without disabilities.

Shattuck et al. (2012) found that young adults with ASD, particularly within the first two years after high school, have a lower rate of employment relative to those diagnosed with speech/language impairment, learning disabilities, or mental retardation. Within the first two years, post high school graduation, less than 50 percent of individuals with ASD were employed or enrolled in postsecondary education.

Hansen (2015) researched the preparedness needs of students with ASD by surveying employers, parents, and college students. Notably, the biggest concerns reported by both employers and parents revolved around social communication issues, including the following: workplace etiquette and norms, reciprocal dialogue, networking skills, personal insight, and nonverbal communication (Hansen, 2015). College students, however, did not see social communication issues as a primary concern. Because theory of mind, which entails placing oneself in someone else's shoes, and social communication are two significant problems for individuals with ASD, these types of workplace issues must be expressly explained. We need better mutual understanding of employer and employee needs for successful integration.

Kaye, Jans, and Jones (2011) noted that a significant amount of prior research showed positive attitudes and success stories regarding the hiring and employment of those with disabilities since the enactment of the American with Disabilities Act. The unemployment rates of individuals with disabilities, however, starkly contrasts this rosy picture. Researchers, therefore, surveyed human resource professionals and managers regarding their opinions as to why other employers fail to hire or retain employees with disabilities, eliminating the dishonesty that may stem from discussing one's own workplace. Of the 468 questionnaires completed, the three primary barriers that arose included (1) ignorance in how to accommodate those with disabilities and the notion they will be a burden; (2) concern over the cost of accommodations (although studies have shown generally inexpensive accommodations); and (3) the threat of legal liability. Also highly noted was continued discrimination. The most highly-endorsed solution for these concerns was increased, high-caliber training for supervisors and managers on disability issues, including exposure to successful employees with disabilities (533-534).

Research conducted by Butterworth et al. (2012) looked at training and mentorship interventions in employment outcomes, noting that training is a key component for employers and employees in ensuring professionals have access to updated knowledge. Additionally, the mentorship component played a large role in successful outcomes due to individualized and tailored support (Butterworth et al. 2012).

Although a few large national chains and small local stores are considered "autism-friendly," the need for widespread employer training, understanding, and acceptance of individuals with ASD is great. "People with autism have unique talents and they can be some of your best employees . . . they don't need to be micromanaged or get special treatment. Simply give them a challenge and the support that they need" ("Work and Autism" 2013).

Socialization

Abnormal social approaches, difficulty with typical back-and-forth conversation, lack of proper social responses, and deficits in verbal and nonverbal communication are at the heart of Autism Spectrum Disorder (American Psychiatric Association, 2013, 27). Most individuals with ASD have a desire to engage in social activities, but social skill deficits make interactions a challenge, which can lead to feelings of loneliness and isolation (Koegel et al. 2013). The program, Playground Partners, developed by Touchstone Behavioral Health, works to improve the communication and socialization of children diagnosed with ASD, ages six to twelve, through playground interaction (Scott 2011). According to Scott (2011), program coordinators collect data prior to and after program implementation, and have seen success with increased interaction and gained friendships. The goal of Playground Partners is to familiarize typically developing children to children with ASD early so that they can increase their understanding of how ASD affects social behavior. This level of inclusion and peer modeling aims to reduce negative perceptions of the diagnosis through early disclosure and practical experiences. The resulting increased understanding of the condition helps to foster communication amongst all students, on and off the playground.

Although many are socially engaged and included in social opportunities in K-12, challenges occur when adults with ASD try to find belonging without structured support. Myers et al. (2015) point out that once individuals with ASD leave the school system, community connections are often lost; teachers, peers, and extracurricular activities that accompany education quickly disappear. Important social skills for adults, such as understanding disguised or nonverbal cues in conversations, are especially difficult to master in the absence of direct support or educational settings (Matthews et al. 2015). Because of this absence of professional support for adults with

ASD, acceptance and inclusivity must come from non-professionals, citizens with the untapped potential and unknown skill sets who can create positive change.

With several previous studies focused on the outcomes of peer networks, Hochman et al. (2015) sought to find the effects of peer interventions on the social engagement of four high school students with ASD interacting at lunchtime with their non-ASD peers. While looking at baseline data, researchers noted the very limited interactions of individuals with ASD during lunchtime. Peers without disabilities may have shown reluctance to speak to those with ASD due to attitudes or stigma attached to the diagnosis, as well as lack of structured opportunities to interact. "The primary barrier to social interaction for students with ASD in this study may have been not social-related skill deficits but, rather, limited structured opportunities to connect with peers without disabilities" (Hochman et al. 2015, 113). Results of the peer networks showed substantial increases in peer interaction and social engagement for all four students, although researchers noted they could not distinguish which parts of the peer networks were responsible for these improvements. Additionally noteworthy, however, is that researchers found peer interaction and socialization were not generalizable to days when no networking was scheduled. This may have been due to non-ASD peers choosing to spend lunch with preferred friends, or not understanding the ability to meet outside of scheduled lunches. Non-ASD peers expressed that they considered their partners with ASD to be their friends at the end of the semester, but those without ASD must further initiate communication to continue development and foster consistent social interaction.

Research conducted by Asselt-Goverts et al. (2014) sought to find differences between the social networks of those with ASD, intellectual disabilities (ID), and the general population. Participants with ASD reported being less satisfied with their social networks as compared to the research reference group. Participants with ASD and ID reported fewer network members than the reference group; those with ASD expressed desire for the expansion of their social networks. For example, a thirty-five-year-old participant with ASD noted, "I long for many more contacts, but there is so much fear if someone actually comes closer that you clam up and it usually goes wrong again. . . . To say things wrong. Not to respond in time. Not to have an answer when it is expected from you" (Asselt-Goverts et al. 2014, 1198).

Research denotes that individuals with ASD rely on others to involve them in community and social opportunities, leaving them potentially poor results if no advocate is present (Myers et al. 2015). Hans Asperger expressed how, amongst his patients, it was often their special interests or skills that would lead to social opportunities (as cited in Howlin 2000, 64). Individuals with ASD often do not possess the skills to develop meaningful close friendships sporadically, but through family coordination of social activities (Myers et al. 2015), or via special interest groups which connect with pervasive interests (Howlin 2000). The Autism Society of America (2014) suggests that individuals with ASD may have luck in finding friendships through clubs revolving around the individual's special interest, because finding those with the same interests in the area can be limited.

A study conducted by Carter et al. (2013) explains that although techniques and communication skills must be expressively taught, we should also place responsibility upon community members who interact with those diagnosed with ASD. Interventions should focus on equipping others with the skills, opportunities, and confidence to interact socially with their coworker, classmate, teammate, or partner with ASD. When there is hesitation or uncertainty about how to interact with someone with ASD, providing basic information and guidance may increase their confidence and capacity to seek out and maintain interactions (Carter et al. 2013). "Absent intentional and coordinated efforts spanning school and community contexts, many adolescents with ASD will struggle to connect to individualized experiences that might enable them to flourish as adults" (Carter et al. 2013, 889). It is crucial to provide opportunities for individuals with ASD to socialize regularly. Community members have a responsibility to spread inclusivity, acknowledge and rebuke myths that perpetuate fearfulness, and provide a welcoming environment.

Independent Living

Individuals with Autism Spectrum Disorder face stigma, limited higher education support, minimal employment opportunities, and difficulty connecting socially—these challenges funnel into issues directly related to independent living skills, often made even more problematic with lack of executive functioning ability. Executive functioning can include things such as organizing, sustaining attention, prioritizing, and maintaining a schedule. "Both paid employment and postsecondary education were associated with better living skills and there was at least some indication that community skills may be related to living independently" (Gray et al. 2014). Because many individuals with autism do not earn college degrees, face unemployment, and lack the skill set to become actively involved to remedy these issues, they face burdening family members to care for them.

Krauss, Seltzer, and Jacobson (2005) collected data regarding the positive and negative effects of co-residence versus out-of-family living on individuals with ASD and their mothers. The families of 133 adults (twenty-two years or older) with ASD were sampled; in eighty-four of the families, the son or daughter lived outside of the family, with the remaining forty-nine individuals with ASD living at home.

For those whose son or daughter lived outside of the home, mothers noted significant positive benefits for the individuals with ASD (56.6%)—particularly reports of personal growth, new skills, and social benefits for their sons or daughters. Families reported fewer benefits for their sons or daughters (34.7%), aside from security, if he or she resided in the family home. Krauss et al. (2005) conveyed that mothers reported positive outcomes for their son or daughter living independently outside the home with ASD, while they told a much more complex story about themselves. Mothers who lived with their son or daughter reported more peace of mind and assurance that their child was cared for, but displayed high strain from the caregiving. In contrast, mothers who did not live with their children reported more free time and less exhaustion, but held deep worries for their child's future. As Field and Hoffman (1999) point out, individuals with ASD face many barriers to become self-determined, a key aspect of living independently. Parents of those with ASD, therefore, hold the extremely important role of providing the opportunities and support for the self-determination of their child. These family members and individuals with ASD need community support to foster this development.

Howlin et al. (2013) note the reliance on aging parents as the primary caregivers for adults with autism is particularly concerning, and efforts to enhance accommodation provision is required. Of the social outcomes presented by Howlin et al. (2013), surveying fifty-eight adults diagnosed with ASD, most participants were rated "poorly" concerning residential status, heavily reliant on others to support their daily lives. From a longitudinal study of eighty-nine participants with ASD from 1991 to 2009, the majority were either living with their parents or were in residential care. More than half (61%) of the individuals were living with their families, with only eight adults living independently (9%) (Gray et al. 2014).

Interestingly, Farley et al. (2009) reported a high rate of positive outcomes regarding independent living in their longitudinal study of adult outcomes with ASD. The sample for this study drew from a unique population, where 94 percent of participants were involved in the Church of Jesus Christ of Latter Day Saints, creating several advantages—a focus on family, along with several weekly, structured social opportunities and yearly mission trips (Farley et al. 2009). The successful independent living outcomes of those studied is likely attributed to the inclusive religious community in Utah. This research may point toward hope that as community members understand and embrace individuals with autism, adults with ASD will see their futures as promising, rather than scary.

The Importance of Training and Becoming an Ally

Allies Supporting Autism Spectrum Diversity aims to provide an understanding of ASD in order to press the importance of citizen involvement in assisting a misunderstood population. Many mental health professionals are looking to involve community members in helping individuals with mental illness through training opportunities. Additionally, social justice inequalities, like LGBTQ discrimination, are proactively combated through trainings on campuses. These initiatives are fruitful in developing awareness and providing citizens with a basic tool belt of knowledge that can provide the confidence and gumption to get involved.

Mental Health First Aid (MHFA) is a program offered across the nation, originally developed by an Australian couple, which seeks to train citizens to recognize symptoms of distress in order to provide immediate reassurance and helpful resources. As Baruchin (2015) notes, trainees range from social workers, to police officers, to doctors, and teachers. One Rhode Island police officer, post MHFA training, recalled a scene where a man with schizophrenia was upset

and breaking things in a public area. Once on the scene, the officer remembered his training, reassuring the man that officers were
there to ensure he received proper help, not to arrest him; he stated
the training made a significant difference in resolving the situation
(Baruchin 2015, 72). As the autism community grows, so should our
community involvement. MHFA is a shining example of the type
of positive change that can infiltrate our businesses, emergency services, schools, and overall public perception.

The inspiration for the Allies Supporting Autism Spectrum Diversity drew from the successful format of the LGBTQ Safe Zone
Trainings. These trainings were created to develop and maintain
supportive environments for LGBTQ (lesbian, gay, bisexual, trans-
gender, and queer/questioning) individuals to express acceptance of
diversity, equality, and inclusion (Gay Alliance 2016), primarily in
school settings. Research regarding the effectiveness of these trainings exists, although it is limited. Byrd and Hays (2013) completed
a study surveying school counselors and counselors in training. An
overall analysis of the Safe Space training on LGBTQ competency
noted a significant relationship between trainees and increased
knowledge, awareness, and skills. Byrd and Hayes (2013) explained,
through their research, that LGBTQ individuals would know effective training reduces homoprejudice and heterosexism, making
schools safer for all students. Evans (2002) and Poynter and Lewis
(2003) assessed the Safe Space Program at Iowa State University
and Duke University. Respondents from both locations noted more
awareness, increased comfort level, and overall improved campus
environment for the LGBTQ community. Additionally, Scher (2008)
reported favorable changes in knowledge and specific attitudes, and
noted positive increases in perceived levels of understanding regarding LBGTQ individuals amongst doctoral students of psychology. Participants also expressed support for mandatory Safe Space
training for incoming students (Scher 2008). Because of the positive

response and results of trainings such as Safe Zone and MHFA, the Allies Supporting Autism Spectrum Diversity training emerged.

Allies Supporting Autism (Photo courtesy of the Marshall University Program for Students with Autism Spectrum Disorder)

The Allies Supporting Autism Spectrum Diversity training has a primary focus to serve and create awareness regarding individuals with Autism Spectrum Disorder—to enable campuses and communities to deepen their support by enhancing understanding of the disorder, discovering strategies known to be helpful, and creating welcoming spaces to foster development. Started in 2015, the ally initiative is already deeply rooted in Marshall University's campus in Huntington, West Virginia. Trainers identify individuals, campus departments, community programs, and local businesses who wish to provide support. The goal is to expand this training nationwide.

In this one-hour interactive training, trainees are provided with a basic understanding of ASD severity levels, common patterns of behavior, and deficits in verbal and nonverbal communication, which often coincide with the diagnosis. Difficulties with theory of mind, sensory overload, stimming, and processing speed are described, while practical tools and methods of support are provided.

Post-training, allies receive a sticker with the Allies Supporting Autism Spectrum Diversity emblem. This emblem is a message to individuals with ASD that those who display it are advocates, are supportive, and are trustworthy. They will know that they can come to these allies for assistance, advice, or just to talk to someone who is considerate of their diagnosis. Trained allies will promote understanding and acceptance of individuals with ASD in their professional and personal lives in order to spread the ally mentality. When applicable, allies should be open to providing employment opportunities for qualified individuals with ASD.

According to the Bureau of Labor Statistics (as cited in Butterworth et al. 2014) West Virginia had the lowest employment rate for individuals who have cognitive disabilities of working age (eighteen to sixty-four) at 16.5 percent. This leaves a significant number of adults with ASD relying on Supplemental Security Income (SSI) Benefits—many of whom do not wish to rely on federal money. In 2005, over sixty-eight thousand disabled West Virginians received SSI (Social Security Office of Policy), and the average check for an individual receiving SSI in 2016 in West Virginia was $733 per month. By incorporating training for our community members regarding how to best support and empower individuals with ASD, we can reduce the number of individuals forced to depend on SSI, weaving this population into the fabric of our community.

As the population of individuals with ASD increases, understanding community and social functioning of the individual is important. Schools, families, caregivers, professionals, and legislators must focus on the outcome that low involvement in community and social opportunities may have on the ASD population (Myers 2015). Societal responsibility must shift—growing numbers of individuals diagnosed with Autism Spectrum Disorder points to the need for more than awareness. We need involvement.

WORKS CITED

Ackles, Laurie, Harold Fields, and Rona Skinner. 2013. "A Collaborative Support Model for Students on the Autism Spectrum in College and University Housing." *The Journal of College and University Student Housing*, 39/40 (2/1): 200-12.

American Psychiatric Association. 2013. "Autism Spectrum Disorder." In *The Desk Reference To the Diagnostic Criteria from DSM-5.* Washington, DC: American Psychiatric Publishing.

Asselt-Goverts, A. E. van, P. J. C. M. Embregts, A. H. C. Hendriks, K. M. Wegman, and J. P. Teunisse. 2015. "Do Social Networks Differ? Comparison of the Social Networks of People with Intellectual Disabilities, People with Autism Spectrum Disorders, and Other People Living in the Community." *Journal of Autism and Developmental Disorders* 45 (5): 1191-1203.

"Social/Relationships." *Autism Society of America.* Last modified April 7, 2014. *http://www.autism-society.org/living-with-autism/autism-through-the-lifespan/adulthood/socialrelationships/.*

Bagatell, Nancy. 2010. "From Cure to Community: Transforming Notions of Autism." Ethos Journal of the Society for Psychological Anthropology 38 (1): 33-55.

Baker, Jeffrey. 2013. "Autism at 70 – Redrawing the Boundaries." *The New England Journal of Medicine* 369 (12): 1089-91.

Baruchin, Aliyah. 2015. "First Aid for Mental Illness Shows Promise." *Scientific American Mind* 26 (2): 69-72.

Brolin, Donn, and Norman Gysbers. 1989. "Career Education for Students with Disabilities." *Journal of Counseling and Development* 68 (2): 155-200.

Butterworth, John, Alberto Migliore, Derek Nord, and Amy Gelb. 2012. "Improving the Employment Outcomes of Job Seekers with Intellectual Disabilities and Developmental Disabilities: A Training and Mentoring Intervention for Employment Consultants." *Journal of Rehabilitation* 78 (2): 20-29.

Butterworth, John, Jean Winsor, Frank Smith, Allison Hall, Alberto Migliore, Jaimie Timmons, and Daria Domin. 2014. "StateData: The National Report on Employment Services and Outcomes." Boston, MA: University of Massachusetts Boston, Institute for Community Inclusion.

Byrd, Rebekah and Danica Hays. 2013. "Evaluating a Safe Space Training for School Counselors and Trainees Using a Randomized Control Group Design." *Professional School Counseling* 17 (1): 20-31.

Cai, Ru Ying and Amanda Richdale. 2016. "Educational Experiences and Needs of Higher Education Students with Autism Spectrum Disorder." *Journal of Autism and Developmental Disorders* 46 (1): 31-41.

Campbell, Fiona .K. 2007. "Exploring Internalized Ableism using Critical Race Theory." *Disability and Society* 23 (2): 151-62.

Campbell, Jonathan. 2006. "Changing Children's Attitudes toward Autism: A Process of Persuasive Communication." *Journal of Developmental Physical Disabilities* 18 (3): 251-72.

Carter, Erik, Michelle Harvey, Julie Taylor, Katherine Gotham. 2013. "Connecting Youth and Young Adults with Autism Spectrum Disorders to Community Life." *Psychology in the Schools* 50 (9): 888-98.

Centers for Disease Control and Prevention. 2015. "Autism Spectrum Disorder (ASD)." Data & Statistics. Last modified July 11, 2016. *http://www.cdc.gov/ncbddd/autism/data.html*.

Donvan, John & Caren Zucker. 2016. *In a Different Key: The Story of Autism*. New York: Crown Publishers.

Ellison, Marc. 2013. "Assessing the Readiness of Higher Education to Instruct and Support Students with Asperger's Disorder." EdD diss., Marshall University.

Evans, Nancy. 2002. "The Impact of an LGBT Safe Zone Project on Campus Climate." *Journal of College Student Development* 43 (4): 522-39.

Farley, Megan, William McMahon, Eric Fombonne, William Jenson, Judith Miller, Michael Gardner, Heidi Block, Carmen Pingree, Edward Ritvo, Riva Ritvo, and Hilary Coon. 2009. "Twenty-year Outcome for Individuals with Autism and Average or Near-Average Cognitive Abilities." *Autism Research* 2 (2): 109-18.

Field, Sharon and Alan Hoffman. 1999. "The Importance of Family Involvement for Promoting Self-Determination in Adolescents with Autism and other Developmental Disabilities." *Focus on Autism and Other Developmental Disabilities* 14 (1):36-41.

"Safe Zone Programs." *GayAlliance.org.* Accessed March 20, 2016. *http:// www.gayalliance.org/programs/education-safezone/safezone-programs/.*

Gillespie-Lynch, Kristen, Patricia Brooks, Fumio Someki, Rita Obeid, Christina Shane-Simpson, Steven Kapp, Nidal Daou, and David Smith. 2015. "Changing College Students' Conceptions of Autism: An Online Training to Increase Knowledge and Decrease Stigma." *Journal of Developmental Disorders* 45: 2553-66.

Gray, Kylie, Caroline Keating, John Taffe, Avril Brereton, Stewart Einfeld, Tessa Reardon, and Bruce Tonge. 2014. "Adult Outcomes in Autism: Community Inclusion and Living Skills." *Journal of Autism Developmental Disorders* 44 (12): 3006-15.

Griffin, Megan, Allison Summer, Elise McMillan, Tammy Day, and Robert Hodapp. 2012. "Attitudes Toward Including Students with Intellectual Disabilities at College." *Journal of Policy and Practice in Intellectual Disabilities* 9 (4): 234-39.

Hansen, Rebecca. 2015. "Understanding Employment Preparedness Needs for College Students with Asperger's Disorder." EdD diss., Marshall University.

Hellemans, Hans, Herbert Roeyers, Wouter Leplae, Tine Dewaele, and Dirk Deboutte. 2006. "Sexual Behavior in High-Functioning Male Adolescents and Young Adults with Autism Spectrum Disorder." *Journal of Autism Developmental Disorders* 28 (2): 93-104.

Hochman, Julia, Erik Carter, Kristen Bottema-Beutel, Michelle Harvey, and Jenny Gustafson. 2015. "Efficacy of Peer Networks to Increase Social Connections among High School Students with and without Autism Spectrum Disorder." *Exceptional Children* 82 (1): 96-116.

Holland, Dorothy, William Lachicotte Jr., Debra Skinner, and Carole Cain. 1998. *Identity and Agency in Cultural Worlds.* Cambridge, MA: Harvard University Press.

Howlin, Patricia. 2000. "Outcome in Adult Life for More Able Individuals with Autism or Asperger Syndrome." *Autism* 4 (1): 63-83.

Howlin, Patricia, Phillipa Moss, Sarah Savage, and Michael Rutter. 2013. "Social Outcomes in Mid- to Later Adulthood among Individuals Diagnosed with Autism and Average Nonverbal IQ as Children." *Journal of the American Academy of Child & Adolescent Psychiatry* 52 (6): 572-81.

Jacoby, Erica. 2015. "Community Perspectives on Autism Spectrum Disorder." MA diss., Ohio State University College.

Kaye, Stephen, Lita Jans, and Erica Jones. 2011. "Why Don't Employers Hire and Retain Workers with Disabilities?" *Journal of Occupational Rehabilitation* 21 (4): 526-36.

Koegel, Lynn, Kristen Ashbaugh, Robert Koegel, Whitney Detar, and April Regester. 2013. "Increasing Socialization in Adults with Asperger's Syndrome." *Psychology in the Schools* 50 (9): 899-909.

Krauss, Marty, M. M. Seltzer, and H.T. Jacobson. 2005. "Adults with Autism Living at Home or in Non-Family Setting: Positive and Negative Aspects of Residential Status." *Journal of Intellectual Disability Research* 49 (2): 111-24.

Ling, Candy, Winnie Mak, and Janice Cheng. 2010. "Attribution Model of Stigma towards Children with Autism in Hong Kong." *Journal of Applied Research in Intellectual Disabilities* 23: 237-49.

Matthews, Nicole, Agnes Ly, and Wendy Goldberg. 2014. "College Students' Perceptions of Peers with Autism Spectrum Disorder." *Journal of Autism and Developmental Disorders* 45 (1): 90-99.

Matthews, Nicole, Christopher Smith, Elena Pollard, Sharman Ober-Reynolds, Janet Kirwan, and Amanda Malligo. 2015. "Adaptive Functioning in Autism Spectrum Disorder during the Transition to Adulthood." *Journal of Autism and Developmental Disorders* 45 (8): 2349-60.

Myers, Emily, Beth Davis, Gary Stobbe, and Kristie Bjornson. 2015. "Community and Social Participation among Individuals with Autism Spectrum Disorder Transitioning to Adulthood. *Journal of Autism and Developmental Disorders* 45 (8): 2373-81.

Poynter, Kerry and E. Lewis. 2003. "SAFE on Campus Assessment Report." *Duke University Center for LGBT Life*. Durham, NC.

Raue, Kimberly and Laurie Lewis. "Students with Disabilities at Degree-Granting Postsecondary Institutions." *U.S. Department of Education, National Center for Education Statistics*. Washington, DC: US Government Printing Office, 2011. PDF.

Roux, Anne M., Paul Shattuck, Benjamin Cooper, Kristy Anderson, Mary Wagner, and Sarah Narendorf. 2013. "Postsecondary Employment Experiences among Young Adults with an Autism Spectrum Disorder." *Journal of the American Academy of Child & Adolescent Psychiatry* 52 (9): 931-39.

Scher, Lauren. 2008. "Beyond Acceptance: An Evaluation of the Safe Zone Project in a Clinical Psychology Doctoral Program." PsyD diss., Long Island University.

Scott, Eugene. 2011. "Program Helps Autistic Kids Benefit from Recess," *AZ Central,* last modified April 6, 2011, *https://owl.english.purdue.edu/owl/resource/717/05/.*

Shattuck, Paul, Sarah Narendorf, Benjamin Cooper, Paul Sterzing, Mary Wagner, and Julie Taylor. 2012. Postsecondary Education and Employment amongst Youth with an Autism Spectrum Disorder. *Pediatrics* 129 (6): 1042–1049.

Social Security Office of Policy. *Social Security and SSI Statistics by Congressional District, December 2002.* Accessed March 20, 2016. *https://www.ssa.gov/policy/docs/factsheets/cong_stats/2002/wv.html.*

Staniland, Jessica and Mitchell Byrne. 2013. The Effects of a Multi-Component Higher-Functioning Autism Anti-Stigma Program on Adolescent Boys. *Journal of Autism Developmental Disorders* 43 (12): 2816-29.

United States Equal Employment Opportunity Commission. "The ADA: Your Responsibilities as an Employer." EEOC.gov, accessed January 10, 2016, *https://www.eeoc.gov/eeoc/publications/ada17.cfm.*

Weiss, Mary Jane, Eliza DelPizzo-Cheng, Robert LaRue, and Kimberly Sloman. 2009. "ABA and PBS: The Dangers in Creating Artificial Dichotomies in Behavioral Intervention." *Behavior Analyst Today* 10 (3–4): 429-439.

"Work and Autism: Your Questions Answered." *CNN.com.* Last modified May 3, 2013, *http://www.cnn.com/2013/05/03/health/autism-chat-irpt/index.html.*

About the Contributors

Hillary Adams, EdD, is the Employment Coordinator for the College Program for Students with Autism Spectrum Disorder. She holds a master's degree in Mental Health Counseling and a doctorate in Education with a focus on Leadership. Adams has worked for the College Program for Students with Autism Spectrum Disorder since 2011. Her research on employer attitudes toward employees with ASD has led to her interest in developing transition skills for students with autism to find meaningful employment. She is focused on creating ties with local and national employers to enhance workplace environments for people with ASD while developing opportunities for graduates. Adams also has a passion for educating community members on best practices for the inclusion and support of individuals with Autism Spectrum Disorder. As a native of Huntington, West Virginia, Adams believes that investing time in the education of citizens on the subject of diversity is vital to the continued growth and altruistic development of the Tri-State area.

Eugenia Damron is an Assistant Professor and Program Director for Leadership Studies, which was her doctoral emphasis. She also received an Education Specialist in Educational Administration, Master's in Preschool Special Needs, and Bachelor's in Special Education, all from Marshall University. Damron has been teaching for over thirty years. Her experiences with students on the autism spectrum range from preschool to college. She has witnessed and advocated for many changes for three decades.

Damron taught preschool special needs, was an elementary principal, Director of Special Education for a six-county region, and now teaches at Marshall University. She also consults with local Christian Schools to ensure that students with special needs are able to attend these schools and experience success despite limitations in special classes or resources provided. Having nurtured relationships with parents and students, she believes that it takes everyone to educate everyone. No child has everything they need without the support and enhancement provided by others. The more we all work together to promote diversity and tolerance, the better our community will be for all people. She believes that a community invested in the inclusion and support of persons on the autism spectrum is a community devoted to all people and their needs. This attitude of acceptance will keep Huntington, West Virginia, on a path towards greatness and will sustain the efforts already made which allowed us to become the recipient of the Best Communities award this year.

BRIAN A. HOEY is a Professor of Anthropology in the Department of Sociology and Anthropology and the Associate Dean of the Honors College at Marshall University. He received his interdisciplinary BA in Human Ecology from the College of the Atlantic and PhD in Anthropology from the University of Michigan. His ethnographic research explores the social, cultural, and personal impacts of economic restructuring through the lens of community development and, in particular, the phenomenon of non-economic migration. In addition to a continuing interest in career change, identity, and the moral meanings of work, Hoey has a longstanding interest in the anthropology of space and place and, in particular, the effects of disaster on human health. Hoey has published on these and other subjects in *American Ethnologist, City and Society, Journal of Appalachian Studies, Journal of Anthropological Research, Journal of Contemporary Ethnography, Ethnology,* several book chapters, and his books *I'm Afraid of that Water* (with E. Lassiter and B. Campbell; West Virginia Univeristy Press, 2020) and *Opting for Elsewhere* (Vanderbilt University Press, 2014). He has been the recipient of fellowships and grants from Fulbright, the Alfred P. Sloan Foundation, and the Oral History Association.

KRISTEN KLAAREN received her BA from Hope College in 1987, her MA from the University of Iowa in 1989, and her PhD in Social Psychology from the University of Virginia in 1993. For the last 23 years, she has taught at Randolph-Macon College, a small liberal arts institution in Ashland, Virginia, where she is currently a Professor of Psychology and Chair of the Psychology Department. A teacher/scholar at heart, she has won several teaching awards, including the Thomas Branch Award for Excellence in Teaching in 1998 and 2000 and the United Methodist Church's Exemplary Teacher Award in 2017. She teaches classes such as Social Psychology, The Psychology of Prejudice, and Psychology and Law. She also co-leads a travel course to South Africa with co-author Scott London. She has published in journals such as *The Journal of Applied Social Psychology, Psychological Science, Personality and Social Psychology Bulletin*, and *Safundi: The Journal of South African and American Comparative Studies*. Her primary research interests are in the area of prejudice and privilege. She and her student collaborators have investigated how and why people confront racist comments, awareness of white privilege, and how best to educate people about discrimination and privilege. Much of her work has taken a multicultural approach, focusing in part on social transformations that have occurred in South Africa. In her collaborative research with Scott London, she explores the ways in which issues of privilege, race, and racism are negotiated in dialogue groups that include diverse groups of South African and American university students.

SCOTT LONDON received his BA from Vassar College and his MA and PhD in Cultural Anthropology from the University of Arizona, and has taught at Randolph-Macon College, a small liberal arts institution in Virginia, since 2001. A dedicated teacher, he teaches courses on cultural anthropology, linguistics, cultures of Africa, and socio-legal studies, as well as a travel course in South Africa with co-author Kristen Klaaren. A legal anthropologist with an interest in gender-based violence, he studied family law and domestic violence in Senegal, West Africa, with support from the National Science Foundation, Fulbright, and the West African Research Association. His research focuses on the negotiation of gender and religious identity in both the family court system and informal family and community-based dispute resolution settings. Currently, he is working on an ethnographic study of campus sexual assault in the United States. In South Africa, he has conducted research on religious identity in African independent churches and on interracial dialogue. In his work with Kristen Klaaren, he examines interactions among South African and American university students to investigate the ways in which cross-cultural context complicates and facilitates interracial dialogue.

HANNAH SMITH received her BS in Biochemistry and BA in Anthropology with a minor in Classical Latin from Marshall University. Smith has presented papers about growing up in West Virginia at the West Virginia Young Writer's Convention, and on the local history and culture of Huntington, West Virginia, at the Southern Anthropological Society (SAS) Annual Conference. She was a student intern of the SAS, assisting in planning the 51st annual conference. She is a co-author on the introductory chapter of this volume. A native of Kenova, West Virginia, in the Huntington/Tri-State area, her passion for Appalachia influenced her to plan the conference, and her love for the state spills over into her research. She is now completing her master's degree in Environmental Management from Duke University in order to return to West Virginia and help the state transition to a future of stable jobs and a sustainable environment through applied research and policy negotiation.

REBECCA L. UPTON is Professor of Sociology and Anthropology at DePauw University, where she is also Director of the Global Health program. She received her PhD in medical anthropology with a background in anthropological demography and population health from Brown University and her MPH degree from the Emory University Rollins School of Public Health, where she is an affiliated faculty member. Her research for the past two decades has focused on the intersections between infertility, reproductive health, and gender in southern Africa. Specifically, she has been working in Botswana and throughout southern Africa on issues of HIV/AIDS, assisted reproductive technologies (ARTs), masculinity, and migration. Her current research utilizes qualitative methods in public health to examine the transnational migration of Tswana women who seek access to health care across state boundaries using social media and other technologies. She has been the recipient of several Fulbright Fellowship awards and grants from the Andrew Mellon and Alfred P. Sloan foundations and has held the Edward Myers Dolan endowed chair in Sociology and Anthropology at DePauw University. She is the author of *The Negotiation of Work, Family and Masculinity Among Christian Long-Haul Truck Drivers: What Would Jesus Haul?* (Lexington Books) and her publications appear in the *Journal of Contemporary Ethnography, Gender and Society, Gender and Development,* the *African Journal of Reproductive Health,* and the *Journal of Southern African Studies,* among others.

MELINDA BOLLAR WAGNER received her PhD in anthropology from the University of Michigan. She is professor emerita of anthropology and Appalachian studies at Radford University in Radford, Virginia, and past president of the Appalachian Studies Association. Wagner has received awards in recognition of innovative undergraduate teaching, having led groups of students in collaborative projects with communities since 1983. For example, students buttressed community efforts at cultural conservation in five counties by undertaking ethnographic study of cultural attachment to land. Most recently, she and her students have turned their attention to the Roots with Wings oral history project, an initiative in place-based education, in cooperation with community partners and public-school teachers. Her work on religion in America has included the ethnographies *Metaphysics in Midwestern America* (Ohio State University Press, 1980) and *God's Schools: Choice and Compromise in American Society* (Rutgers University Press, 1990).

www.ingramcontent.com/pod-product-compliance
Lightning Source LLC
Chambersburg PA
CBHW020612270326
41927CB00005B/295